METHODOLOGY
OF MATHEMATICAL ECONOMICS AND ECONOMETRICS

METHODOLOGY
OF MATHEMATICAL ECONOMICS
AND ECONOMETRICS

By GERHARD TINTNER

THE UNIVERSITY OF CHICAGO PRESS

CHICAGO & LONDON

This book is also issued as Vol. II, No. 6, of the *International Encyclopedia of Unified Science,* published by The University of Chicago Press.

Library of Congress Catalog Card Number: 67–30130

THE UNIVERSITY OF CHICAGO PRESS, CHICAGO & LONDON

The University of Toronto Press, Toronto 5, Canada

For

LÉONTINE, PHILLIP
CINDY, and HEIDI

Preface

In this essay I have attempted to present some methodological problems of mathematical economics and econometrics, and also of operations research (econometrics of enterprise), to a public which does not necessarily consist of economists. Hence, it has been impossible to treat the whole field, and the selection of topics may be found to be one-sided.

Mathematical economics is the use of mathematics in the construction of economic models. Econometrics may be defined as the utilization of mathematics, economics, and statistics in an effort to evaluate economic models empirically with the help of concrete data and to investigate the empirical support of certain economic theories.

I also have to apologize for sometimes presenting the results of my own research. My excuse is that I am, of course, more familiar with these particular problems and hence able to discuss them more adequately than the results established by others. I concede, however, that a diligent search might have discovered more suitable examples. But the literature is so extensive and has become so specialized that more time and effort would have been expended than I felt I could spare.

It seems to me that it would be fruitless to engage in long philosophical discussions of some of the methodological issues which have bedeviled the enormous literature in this field. Instead, I have tried to present various views on those questions together with some simple examples — a method which should enable the reader to form his own opinions on such questions as the suitability of mathematics, the possibility of measurement in economics, the various views on probability, some aspects of economic prediction, and so on. If the reader desires more information, he is referred to the literature cited.

All these questions, in my opinion, are far from settled, and this essay might be considered a progress report which endeavors to present the contemporary status of some of the more important methodological problems. I hope that it will stimulate interest among those who are not economists, especially mathematicians and natural scientists, in the problem of modern mathematical economics and econometrics. A valuable survey of almost the entire field of mathematical economics may be found in the two books of R. G. D. Allen (1949, 1963). For a simple introduction to the mathematical and statistical methods used, I might refer the reader to my own books (Tintner 1952*b*, 1960*c*, 1962) and to Kemeny, Snell, and Thompson (1957), which also contain a great many practical applications of econometric methods to concrete economic data.

I am much obliged to the National Science Foundation, Washington, D.C., for financial support. I also want to thank Aurelius Morgner, Department of Economics, University of Southern California, for bibliographical help.

I thank Rudolf Carnap and Charles Morris for helpful advice and criticism of a first version of this work. Also, I would like to thank a number of my friends and colleagues for critical remarks: M. Bronfenbrenner (Pittsburgh), W. W. Cooper (Pittsburgh), C. R. Fayette (Lyons), E. Fels (Munich), N. Georgescu-Roegen (Nashville, Tennessee), T. Haavelmo (Oslo), B. Higgins (Austin, Texas), C. Humphrey (Los Angeles), T. W. Hutchison (Birmingham, England), K. Kimura (Nagoya), F. Machlup (Princeton), C. McConnell (Los Angeles), R. N. Narayanan (New Haven), J. B. Nugent (Los Angeles), J. Pfanzagl (Cologne), H. Wold (Uppsala). I am obliged to R. Watson (Los Angeles) for computational help.

G. T.

LOS ANGELES

Contents

I. Introduction

This monograph deals with some of the fundamental methodological problems of mathematical economics and econometrics. We start with a definition of economics. But the word of Cairnes (1875, p. 148), one of the outstanding older writers on economic methodology, should be remembered: "Definitions in the present state of economic science should be regarded as provisional only, and may be expected to need constant revision and modification with the progress of economic knowledge." Economics has changed much in the past, and continues to change very fast. Hence, the words of Cairnes are as true now as when they were written.

Economics has been defined as the science which studies human behavior as a relationship between ends and scarce means which have alternative uses (Robbins 1949, p. 16) or, on the other hand, as the science of administration of scarce resources in human society (Lange, 1953). A more recent definition by the same author (Lange 1963, p. 1) reads: "Political economy, or social economy, is the study of social laws governing the production and distribution of the material means of satisfying human needs."

Economics has a long history, dating back to Plato and Aristotle (Schumpeter 1954) or even earlier (Bernadelli 1961). It would be useless to deny that the bulk of the results of theoretical economics has been achieved without mathematical means. Mathematical economics, which also has a long history, has only recently come into prominence.

In theoretical economics we construct fundamental models which we try to apply to concrete economic problems. The necessity of economic theory, which was denied by the historical school in Germany and by the institutionalist school in the United States, is now almost universally recognized. This, however, is not true in regard to the use of the method of mathematics in economics (L. von Mises 1949, pp. 347 ff., 697 ff.,

1

706 ff.; see also Georgescu-Roegen 1966, p. 49). The repudiation of the anti-theoretical schools of German historicism and American institutionalism should, however, not imply that the study of economic history and of economic institutions is useless and should be neglected. Also, it need not be claimed that mathematical economics and econometrics are the *only* methods for the study of problems in economics (Tintner 1952, p. 13).

No one can deny that economics holds a special position among the social sciences. It has perhaps reached a degree of scientific maturity that is still lacking in many of the other social sciences. Nevertheless, the scientific achievement of economics is not yet comparable to that of modern physics or genetics. Georgescu-Roegen (1965) attributes this limited success of economics to the nature of many economic models, which are constructed after the example of classical physics. The implied conditions of measurability and linearity are not always fulfilled. There is much to this criticism, and we shall come back to some of these problems. It remains to be seen whether stochastic models of the economy will be more successful.

Some of the fundamental difficulties of modern mathematical economics have also been pointed out by Georgescu-Roegen (1966, pp. 49 ff.). In economics we frequently, perhaps always, deal with phenomena which are qualitative and which we can quantify only imperfectly. The qualitative residual shows itself then in non-linearities of the relations between quantified phenomena.

I believe, however, that some (but not all) of our difficulties in mathematical economics (especially in utility theory and the theory of choice) are of our own making. Modern physics has shown that the number of ultimate particles (whatever these may be) is large but finite. Similarly, whereas subjective time may be continuous, any measured clock time is also discontinuous. Many of the difficulties connected with set and measure theory disappear when we deal with finite aggregates. Hence we should properly use only difference equations, and those we use in mathematical economics and elsewhere are convenient idealizations. (Kemeny, Snell, and Thompson 1957).

2

First, let us examine a spirited criticism of modern economics which emphasizes some of its difficulties. Schoeffler (1955, pp. 17 ff.) in a critical study points to many weaknesses existing in contemporary economics. Mechanical behavior models, like the theory of the firm, may be called artificial mechanization. Batteries of homogeneous active agents — for example, a competitive industry — may lead to artificial simplification. The empirical behavior equation — for example, the consumption function (consumption explained by income) — is an artificial generalization. Classification and description by types — for example, classification of firms into industries — may be called artificial systematization. Mapping of structural elements of the world — for example, production surfaces (production explained in terms of various factors of production, such as capital and labor) — may be artificial fixation. Times series analysis, like analysis into trend, business cycle, and seasonal components, may imply artificial factorization. Endogenous models — for example, certain business cycle models which explain the cycle without assuming outside influences — may lead to artificial closure. Semi-endogenous models, which also include exogenous variables — those which influence the system but are not influenced by it — may encompass artificial semiclosure. Partial consideration of variables — the tendency to consider only economic or perhaps closely related effects of policy measures — may be artificial isolation. Assumptions verified by their logical consequences — for example, when the economist tests his hypotheses not directly by opinion surveys but with the help of available statistical series — may lead to artificial indirectness.

I believe that few economists would deny the cogency of much of this criticism. It shows, however, only that, considerable as the achievements of contemporary economics are, they are still far from complete.

The success of econometrics depends, of course, upon the availability of good data (Morgenstern 1963), but our models also need improvements. Until the theoretical problem of oligopoly (a few sellers in a market with many consumers) is solved, there is little hope that we can achieve somewhat realistic results in a country like the United States, where oligopoly in many important markets is the prevailing form of organization. Oligopoly is a situation different from free competition (many sellers and buyers) and monopoly (one seller and many buyers).

Since there are few sellers and many buyers in an oligopolistic market (Baran and Sweezy, 1966; Shonfield 1965), even the economic models of statics are seen to be deficient. Economic statics is defined by Hicks (1946, p. 115):

> I call economic statics those parts of economic theory where we do not trouble about dating; economic dynamics those parts where every quantity must be dated. For example, in economic statics we think of an entrepreneur employing such-and-such quantities of factors and producing with their aid such-and-such quantities of products, but we do not ask when the factors are employed and when the products come to be ready.

If time is introduced, the difficulties multiply. An interesting discussion of the semantic confusion in economics is that of Machlup (1963). Papandreou (1958) investigates the structure of economics from the point view of modern mathematical logic and semantics. His analysis stresses the theoretical shortcomings of many economic theories and models.

The progress of economics has been slow because of the influence of ideological bias and some ancient metaphysical ideas which have long been discarded in the more mature natural sciences. Ideology is well defined by Robinson (1962, p. 8): "What then are the criteria of an ideological proposition opposed to a scientific one? First, that if an ideological proposition is treated in a logical manner, it either dissolves into a completely meaningless noise or turns out to be a circular argument." (See also Topitsch 1958, 1961.) Perhaps it should be recognized that "ideology" is a very ill-defined and much abused word of uncertain meanings (Quine 1960).

It is certainly understandable (even if deplorable) that in the past and in the present, on the left and on the right, economists have been very much influenced by the ideological struggles of their time and have sometimes illegitimately presented value judgments as scientic truth. This is perhaps unavoidable. Nobody will be concerned with economics who is not vitally interested in social matters and is not looking for solutions of burning social problems. Until recently, with few exceptions, the intellectual level of discussion of economic matters and the standards in this field were not high. More gifted intellectuals were (and perhaps still are) attracted to the natural sciences and mathematics. These fields, it must be confessed, are certainly intellectually much more attractive, and the danger of purely ideological influences is perhaps smaller there.

Topitsch (1958, pp. 235 ff.; 1961) has emphasized the importance of the idea of natural right in classical political economy (Adam Smith and his school). The same is also true of Schumpeter (1954, pp. 122 ff.). It cannot be denied that traces of this empty idea are still to be found in contemporary economic writings. Topitsch shows how since antiquity social phenomena and organizations (e.g., government, the state) have been used to explain natural phenomena. They are interpreted as "natural laws," and the natural laws are then used in turn to explain other social phenomena. In the course of history they have become empty formulas and have been used to justify conservative, liberal, and socialist ideas.

Both the Physiocrats and the classical British school of economists base themselves largely upon this empty concept of natural law. Hence early economic writings are almost completely normative. In spite of this ideological orientation, there are of course important scientific contributions made by the physiocratic and classical school of economics. This ideological influence also explains in part the famous "invisible hand" of Adam Smith, which makes selfish ends promote the common good (Viner 1927; see also Wicksell 1934, pp. 72 ff.) We should not forget, however, as has been emphasized by Robbins (1961), that the English classical economists were not *uncritical* advocates of laissez-faire. This is true even of Hume, Adam Smith, Bentham, Malthus, Ricardo, and of the writings of J. S. Mill, which constitute in a sense the great synthesis of the classical system. In disagreement with Schumpeter (1954), who stressed the novelty and undeniable contributions of the marginal revolution, especially the Austrian school, I would like to emphasize the continuity of the classical tradition in economics, stressed by Marshall (1948). It is particularly evident in the development of economics after the death of Schumpeter. Economists who deal with the problems of economic development are rediscovering many ideas of the English classical school of economics, especially those of Malthus and Ricardo. (Baumol 1959). Hence, perhaps it is also not surprising that economists working in the field of economic development make use of Marxist models (Morishima 1954, Robinson 1949). It has also been pointed out recently by Chipman (1965) that the English classical writers anticipated many of the results which were later established by modern mathematical economists with the help of advanced mathematical methods.

In the social sciences, just as much as in the natural sciences, we must distinguish between the often ideological and metaphysical motivations of a given thinker and his real scientific contributions. The scientific contributions of Newton do not depend fundamentally upon his peculiar theology and metaphysics, even if they are perhaps partly motivated by these ideas. But it must be confessed that the task of separating ideology and scientific contribution of many of the most famous economists is much more difficult. It is true that economics, like all social sciences, deals with human action. This fact, however, should not prevent us from trying to apply the fundamental scientific methods used elsewhere. The difficulty should not be denied, as has been recently emphasized by Georgescu-Roegen (1966, pp. 3–132). But why has economics not yet been more successful in these endeavors? One source of our difficulty, emphasized by Morgenstern (1963), is the deficiency in much of economic statistics. But the strictly theoretical difficulties are also very great. We find in recent economic literature an undue emphasis on purely static models of a competitive economy. These static models are such that the quantities involved are undated. Free competition prevails in markets with many buyers and sellers. Static competitive models are plainly insufficient for application to economic reality (which is essentially

non-static and also involves many elements of monopoly, oligopoly, and so on).

The work on dynamic models which has flourished in recent
years (Morishima 1964) shows that the fundamental theoretical difficulties connected with economic development have not
been mastered. It is doubtful if the application of the theory
of stochastic processes, which has been advocated, will be
more successful (Sengupta and Tintner 1963, 1964; Mukherjee
et al. 1964; Tintner and Patel 1966).

One weakness of present-day economics, which has been emphasized by Georgescu-Roegen (1960), consists in the fact that
almost all modern economics is strongly related to the analysis
of the competitive phase of modern capitalism. This prevents
economists from coming to grips with pre-capitalist structures,
which are still important in underdeveloped countries (T. W.
Schultz 1964; Georgescu-Roegen 1960). But also, in spite of
some progress in the analysis of non-competitive capitalist structures (J. Robinson 1938; E. H. Chamberlin 1948; Fellner 1959),
these ideas have never been really well integrated into a comprehensive system of economic equilibrium. Bowley (1924) is
almost the only modern writer who has at least tried to include
monopoly (one seller, many buyers) and bilateral monopoly
(one seller, one buyer) into a system of general economic equilibrium. The outstanding problem in mature capitalist economies is, however, really oligopoly (few sellers, many buyers)
and similar structures (Shubik 1959; Baran and Sweezy 1966).
Another difficulty with economics is what Schumpeter (1954)
has called the "Ricardian vice." He says of Ricardo (pp. 472–
73):

His interest was in the clear-cut result of direct, practical significance.
In order to get this he cut this general system to pieces, bundled up as
large parts as possible, and put them in cold storage — so that as many
things as possible should be frozen and "given." He then piled one sim-
plifying assumption upon another, until, having really settled everything
by these assumptions, he was left with only a few aggregative variables
between which, given these assumptions, he set up simple, one-way relations so that, in the end, the desired results emerged almost as tautologies.

This Ricardian vice was, unfortunately, not confined to Ricardo and his immediate disciples. Schumpeter (p. 1171) attributes it with some justice even to Keynes.

The case of Marx is extremely interesting. Topitsch (1961, p. 252) convincingly shows the way in which ancient gnostic and even cabalistic speculations were transmitted to Hegel and from Hegel to Marx. The main idea is the concept of dialectics (Popper 1963*b*) with its scheme of thesis, antithesis, and synthesis, which again in its long historical career became a perfectly empty formula, useful for any purpose. This method of analysis, used by Hegel for the justification of the existing Prussian state (Popper 1957), was used by the Hegelian Marx for the purposes of the revolutionary socialist movement. Again, in spite of the fact that a large portion of the thought of Marx is ideological (or at least motivated by ideology), he is by no means a negligible figure in the history of economics, as Schumpeter (1951*a*) has shown (see Sievers 1962). Recently Georgescu-Roegen (1966, pp. 3–132) has argued that "dialectical" concepts are useful and may even be indispensable in economics. There can be no doubt that he is right in stating that many concepts and ideas in economics, especially in economic policy, are imprecise and vague, in some sense pre-scientific. But since the concrete problems are pressing, we must by necessity use imperfect and not well-delimitated concepts in our discussion. The introduction of dialectial concepts should be welcomed as perhaps the beginning of a serious discussion between Marxist and "standard" (modern non-Marxist) economists (see also Bronfenbrenner 1965).

Whatever his ideological and metaphysical motivations, in economics Marx appears as one of the most important members of the British classical school of economics, extending from Adam Smith to John Stuart Mill (Schumpeter 1951*a*). His thinking must be understood in terms of the fundamental conceptions of this school, which, in spite of progress in many fields, are still largely the fundamental ideas of modern economics (Lange 1963). It is no wonder that Marx, as an economic thinker, now enjoys a certain renaissance and that as conservative an economist as Schumpeter is deeply indebted to Marx. In recent years, in view of the understandable concern of contemporary economists over problems of economic development, one of the most important subjects of the classics — "magnificent dynamics" (Baumol 1959; Hicks 1965) — has brought back certain Marxist concepts which may prove fruitful in our endeavor to understand the process of economic development (J. Robinson 1949, 1962; Morishima 1964; Bronfenbrenner 1965).

Concerning ideological bias, we might well agree with Schumpeter (1951*b*, pp. 280–81):

> There is little comfort in postulating, as has been done sometimes, the existence of detached minds that are immune to ideological bias and ex hypothesi able to overcome it. . . . There is more comfort in the observation that no economic ideology lasts forever and that, with a likelihood that approximates certainly we eventually grow out of each . . . But this still leaves us with the result, some ideology will always be with us, and so, I feel convinced, it will.

That ideological influences are recognized even among Marxists is shown by Lange (1963, pp. 338–9): "At one period in the building of socialism political economy was fettered by dogmatism and by a tendency to transform science into apologetics. This was connected with Stalin's system of the 'cult of personality.'" In an extremely interesting book (Baran and Sweezy 1966), two American Marxists have given a penetrating (but one-sided) analysis of the economy of the United States. This book is especially remarkable for discarding many preconceptions of Marx (and Lenin) and using some ideas and techniques of 'modern' or 'standard' (non-Marxist) economics. May we hope that this example will be followed by Russian, Chinese, and other economists in Communist countries? May we also hope that at least some economists in the non-Communist world will follow this example in the opposite direction and try to learn something from Marxist economics and the experience of planning in the Communist world?

We cannot do better than quote one of the outstanding Marxist economists of our time on the subject of the objectivity of economics:

> Our conclusion about the objectivity of economic science may seem startling. Economists are rather notorious for being unable to reach agreement and for being divided into opposing "schools of thought", "orthodox, and unorthodox," "bourgeois" and "socialist," and many others. The existence of profound disagreement among economists, however, does not refute our thesis about the objectivity of economics as a science. The disagreements can all be traced to one or more of the following sources: 1) Disagreements about social objectives. This is the most frequent source of disagreement, but acts as such only as long as it is implicit and unrecognized. If the social objectives are stated explicitly, the disagreement disappears. For any given set of social objectives and with given assumptions as to empirical conditions, conclusions are drawn with interpersonal validity by the rules of logic and verification. (2) Disagreements about facts. Such disagreements can always be resolved by further observation and study of empirical material. Frequently, however, the empirical data necessary to resolve the disagreement are unavailable. In such cases the issue remains unsettled. The conclusion that the issue cannot be settled with the data available has interpersonal validity. Agreement is reached to withhold judgment. (3) Failure to abide by the rules of logic, of identification and verification. The disagreement can be removed by correct application of the rules. (Lange 1953, p. 749.)

In order to bridge the gap between theoretical concepts and empirical observations, it is necessary to have a procedure of identification, which contains rules establishing the correspondence between the two. This concept of identification introduced by Lange has nothing to do with identification in econometrics discussed below.

There should be no doubt of the fundamental methodological unity of the social and natural sciences:

> There are no other methods or aims in the social and cultural sciences than exist in the natural sciences: observation, description, 'measurement, statistics, the discovery of explanatory laws and theories — more difficult of achievement in the former than in the latter — are the basic procedures. The role of sympathetic "understanding" or "empathy" as a practical guide is certainly not to be minimized, but its results, if they are to be scientifically valid, are subject to the very same objective tests as are the results of inorganic science. . . . To what extent sociology, economics or history are capable of discovering reliable laws on some

level of concept formation is an empirical question and therefore cannot be decided *a priori* on logical grounds. (Feigl 1949, p. 22).

As Carnap (1938) has pointed out, the procedures of social and hence economics are fundamentally the same as in the natural sciences (see also Morris 1938, 1946).

Prices, and quantities sold, interest rates, and the like are all quantitative concepts. Prices are measured in monetary units — for example, dollars. Quantities are measured in pounds, kilograms, or number of items, and so on. Interest rates are given in per cent. For investigations of a whole economy, it is frequently necessary to construct index numbers — for example, a cost-of-living index, various price indexes which represent prices in sectors of the total economy (for example, an index of prices of producers' goods). These problems involve the difficulties of aggregation, which will be discussed below. The economic magnitudes can be observed, and indeed it is the task of economic statistics to give the economist quantitative information about them. Censuses give more or less complete information and sample surveys give information derived by the methods of modern sampling.

But the psychological dispositions of consumers, entrepreneurs, and so on are also of great importance. Consider a farmer who produces a commodity which has a definite period of production. Then his rational action at the time of starting the production process will depend not on the existing price of the commodity in question but on the price he anticipates to prevail when the process of production is complete. Here again, sample surveys will give us more information about anticipated prices, business conditions, and the like (Theil 1961; Katona *et al.* 1954).

For emphasis on the unity of scientific methods in the natural and social sciences we quote Popper (1957, pp. 130 ff.):

. . . I am going to propose a doctrine of the unity of method; that is to say, the view, that all theoretical or generalizing sciences make use of the same method, whether they are natural or social sciences. . . . I do not intend to assert that there are no differences whatever between the methods of the theoretical sciences of nature and of society; such differences clearly exist. . . . But I agree with Comte and Mill and with many others, such as C. Menger, that the methods in the two fields are fundamentally the same. . . . The methods always consist in offering deductive casual explanations, and in testing them (by way of predictions). This has sometimes been called the hypothetical-deductive method, or more often the method of hypothesis, for it does not achieve absolute certainty for any of the scientific statements which it tests; rather, these statements always retain the character of tentative hypotheses, even though their character of tentativeness may cease to be obvious after they have passed a great number of severe tests.

Popper (1957, pp. 136–37) maintains the unity of method in the social and natural sciences against Hayek (1952, p. 140) and even claims that social science is less complicated than physics.

The subject of human action in economics is sometimes called praxeology. It has made much progress in recent years, and many methods connected with it will be discussed below. It is here that the application of modern mathematical methods has been most successful, especially in connection with operations research, the econometrics of enterprise. It is interesting that both the extreme proponent of laissez-faire L. von Mises and the Marxist Lange define praxeology in similar terms. Von Mises (1949, p. 39) says: "The real thing, which is the subject matter of praxeology, human action, stems from the same source as human reasoning. . . . Praxeology conveys exact and precise knowledge of real things." Lange (1963, pp. 188–89) says: "In view of the fact that rationality of action is now a feature of many fields of human activity, there arises the problem of discovering what is that that is common to all fields of rational activity. This has led to the general study of rational activity, *praxeology.*" Lange goes on to include operations research, cybernetics, decision theory, and the marginal calculus in the field of praxeology.

Praxeological methods (econometrics, operations research, cybernetics, programing, and so on) have been used in the United States mainly for military planning and rational planning of private enterprise (Churchman *et al.*, 1957; Dantzig 1963; Vadja 1961; Heady and Candler 1958; Holt *et al.* 1960).

In communist countries they have been used for central planning (O. Lange 1959; Kantorovich 1963). The planning models of certain West European countries (Theil 1961, 1964; Massé 1959; Lesourne 1960) and India (Mahalanobis 1955) deal with mixed economic systems, which in a sense are intermediate between free enterprise and pure collectivism.

II. Mathematical Economics

Economics uses the "logical-deductive" method and derives conclusions from certain fundamental assumptions or axioms, such as rationality and profit maximization. The status of these fundamental postulates is somewhat in doubt (Machlup 1955). We owe to Koopmans (1957, pp. 132 ff.) an interesting discussion of the postulational structure of economic theory. He criticized the ideas of Robbins (1949) and Friedmann (1953), two economists who were similar in their political views — both were ardent advocates of extreme laissez-faire. But Lord Robbins had great confidence in the introspectively established postulate of a preference ordering. He believed that it was possible to derive from this ordering practically the whole of economic theory, perhaps including certain policy recommendations. In contrast Friedmann, who would agree with the position Robbins held on policy, insisted on the view that the fundamental postulates of economics were irrelevant and that only their consequences were testable. The assumptions need not be realistic.

Against Robbins' views, Koopmans maintains that the assumption of a complete and invariable preference ordering contradicts some well-known facts in actual economic choice. Against Friedmann, Koopmans insists that direct verification of the postulates by their consequences is hardly ever possible in economics by experimentation. The indirect verifications involve a lengthy and perhaps uncertain chain of reasoning. Koopmans (1957, p. 142) says: "The theories that have become dear to us can very well stand by themselves as an impressive and highly valuable system of deductive thought, erected on a few premises that seem to be well chosen first approximations to a complicated reality."

A more liberal point of view about the status of economic theory is that of Blaug (1962, p. 606):

A "theory" is not to be condemned merely because is as yet untestable; not even if it is so formed as to preclude testing, provided it draws attention to a significant problem and provides a framework for its discussion from which a testable implication may some day emerge. It cannot be denied that many so-called "theories" in economics have no substantive content and serve merely as filing systems for organizing empirical information. To demand the removal of all heuristic postulates and theorems in the desire to press the principle of verifiability to the limit is to proscribe further research in many branches of economics. It is perfectly true that economists have often deceived themselves — and their readers — by engaging in what Leontief called "implicit theorizing," presenting tautologies in the guise of substantive contributions to economic knowledge. But the remedy for this practice is clarification of purpose, not radical and possibly premature surgery.

The use of mathematics in economics has been criticized not only by anti-theoretical schools like the German historical school and the American institutionalists but also by some writers who emphasize the use of economic theory (L. von Mises 1949; Stigler 1949). Against these views we might quote the opinion of a recognized specialist on the methodology of economics: "On the whole, we arrive at the conclusions, first, that political economy involves conceptions of a mathematical nature requiring to be analyzed in a mathematical spirit; and secondly, that there are certain departments of the science in which valuable aid may be derived from the actual employment of symbolical or diagrammatical methods." (J. N. Keynes 1955, p. 267). One of the founders (Jevons 1911, p. xxiii) of the modern marginal utility theory has this to say: "I hold then, that to argue mathematically, whether correctly or incorrectly, constitutes no real differentia as regards writers on the theory of economics. But it is one thing to argue and another thing to understand and to recognize explicitly the method of argument."

Norbert Wiener (1964, p. 90), whose work in cybernetics has also been most stimulating in economics, is critical: "The mathematics that the social scientists employ and the mathematical physics that they use as their models are the mathematics and mathematical physics of 1850. An econometrician will develop an elaborate and ingenuous theory of demand and supply, inventories and unemployment, and the like, with a relative or total indifference to the methods by which these elusive quantities are observed or measured." This statement by one of the greatest mathematicians of our time cannot be dismissed lightly, since it points to certain definite weaknesses in contemporary mathematical economics and econometrics which no doubt exist. It is perhaps too early to say whether the explicit introduction of stochastic processes into the treatment of economic problems will yield more reliable results (Tintner, Sengupta, and Thomas 1966).

We should deal here with some of the objections against mathematical economics and econometrics by the eminent Austrian economist L. von Mises (1949, pp. 347–54, 374–76, 697–98, 706–11). According to von Mises, the numerical results of econometrics lack universal validity, are essentially historical, and always refer to a given country and a given (past) time period.

We must concede that economics has not yet derived universal laws and constants like physics. Perhaps the only possible exception is the controversial Pareto distribution of incomes (Pareto 1927; Davis 1941, pp. 28 ff.). Discussion of this subject has recently been resumed (Mandelbrot 1960; Steindl 1965). Pareto stated that personal income (at least for higher incomes) follows the law

$$N = Ax^{-B}; \qquad (1)$$

where N is the number of persons receiving income x or more; A and B are constants, and B is about $+1.5$. Now it is possible to derive this law from a specific stochastic process (Champernowne 1953; Mandelbrot 1960; Simon 1957, pp. 145–64; Klein 1962, pp. 140 ff.; Steindl 1965). The matter cannot yet be considered settled, but some empirical investigations contained in the literature give us hope that the Pareto law (perhaps in a slightly more complicated form) might be valid at least as a somewhat crude approximation of many economic phenomena.

But are the specific results of econometric research useless, since they evidently refer to a given country and a given time period? The Swedish econometrician Wold (Wold and Jureén

1953, pp. 307 ff.) has derived demand functions for a number of consumer's goods for the period 1921–39. A demand function explains the quantity demanded of a given commodity in terms of prices and money income. He compares predictions based upon these demand functions with actual consumption of the commodities in Sweden in 1950, as shown in Table 1.

TABLE 1

WOLD'S COMPARISON OF PREDICTIONS OF DEMAND FUNCTIONS
AND OBSERVED COMMODITY CONSUMPTION
(Percentage Change)

Commodity	Predicted	Observed
Milk and cream.	+7	+2
Consumer milk	+1	+6
Butter and margarine	+11	+26
Butter.	+7	+28
Margarine	+16	+23
Cheese.	+13	+12
Eggs.	+6	+42
Meat	+1	+3
Meat (excluding pork).	−3	−13
Pork.	+6	+20
Wheat and rye flour.	−11	−10
Sugar (refined)	+12	+11
Potatoes	−7	−6

This econometric investigation is based upon the following version of the theory of demand: The quantity demanded for a given good is influenced by the price of this commodity and income. The quantity demanded is consumption per head of population; the price is the real price — that is, the money price divided by a consumer price index. Also, income is real income per head — that is, money income divided by the consumers price index.

To appreciate the comparison, it should be realized that Sweden rationed many foodstuffs during the war, and rationing was not abolished until 1949. The prediction depends upon relationships based on family surveys and market statistics collected in Sweden. It is derived from a model which assumes that only price and income changes influence consumption.

A similar analysis is by Fox (1958). He investigates price changes of 30 agricultural commodities, based upon an econo-

17

metric analysis with data taken from statistics in the United States 1922–41. These examples show, however, only that predictions based upon econometric methods are sometimes successful. The econometric method does not guarantee that this will always be the case. If, for example, the relationships investigated show a change in time, it is ideally up to the economist to construct a "dynamic" theory which will explain the very change, but it should not be denied that our dynamic theories are still insufficient.

Another use of econometrics is the "verification" of economic theories. May I here refer to one of my own investigations. It is well known that the celebrated general theory of Keynes (1936), which in a sense has revolutionized economics and was important for the economic policy of various countries, assumes that the (static) supply function of labor depends upon money wages and not upon real wages — that is, money wages divided by the cost of living index. By the supply function of labor, we mean the relationship between the amount of labor offered or supplied as a function of wages, either money wages or real wages. The supply of labor is here measured as the sum of the number of workers employed plus the number of insured unemployed. The wage index is computed as the weighted average of sixteen industries. This gives us an index of money wages. Real wages are computed as the ratio between money wages and a cost of living index. I have investigated this question empirically, using data for British industry 1920–38 (Tintner 1952, pp. 143 ff.). The result of the econometric investigation using various mathematical models is as follows. A statistical test of the fitted relations indicates that it is probable that the supply of British industrial labor in the interwar period depended upon real wages rather than upon money wages alone. This result is of course dependent upon a number of assumptions. The model must be at least approximately valid; the errors must be approximately normally distributed, independent over time, and so on.

The investigation yields an estimate of the elasticity of British labor supply in relation to real wages. This elasticity is estimated as —0.19. Under the assumptions mentioned, it is statistically significant. Hence, if *ceteris paribus* the real wage of industrial labor in Great Britain increases by 1 per cent, we might expect that the supply of labor will decrease by about 0.2 per cent. The negative estimate of the elasticity of supply for labor agrees with economic theory (Bowley 1924, p. 40) and also with empirical results for the United States (Mosback 1959). This negative elasticity of the supply of labor can be explained in the following way. As real wages increase, there will at the same time be a decrease of the number of people who are willing to supply labor. This means that, for example, the number of working wives will decrease, some children will continue their schooling instead of trying to enter the labor market, and so on. This example should be carefully interpreted. It perhaps tells us something about the conditions of the supply of industrial labor in Great Britain during the period investigated, but nothing (except by analogy) about the character of the supply of labor in other countries and in other periods. Nevertheless, it could be used to tentatively question the Keynesian assumption that the demand for labor depends upon money wages and not upon real wages. If the results of the investigation are somewhat reliable, at least the *universal* validity of this fundamental assumption must be questioned.

Problems of Measurability

It has been maintained that some important economic magnitudes cannot be measured (Painlevé 1960; Georgescu-Roegen 1966, pp. 114 ff.). It is evident that many important economic concepts (consumption, production, labor, interest rates, prices) are quantitative. For instance, consumption of specific commodities is given in terms of pounds and number of items. Production of various commodities is again in quantitative form — pounds, number of items. Labor can be measured in terms of days or hours worked. Interest rates are expressed in percentages. Prices appear in dollars. There is perhaps only one important exception which appears in modern but not in classical (and Marxian) economics — satisfaction or utility (Alt 1936;

Pfanzagl 1959). The problem of anticipations and expectations will be discussed below.

Let us consider the static theory of choice (Tintner 1955). Assume that a given individual is faced with the choice among three combinations of goods and services, which we denote by A, B, and C. Without the use of mathematics, the adherents of the Austrian school establish that a rational individual will act as follows. If he does not prefer A to B and also not B to C, he will not prefer A to C. We follow the example of Arrow (1963), Stone (1951), and von Wright (1963a) and introduce a relation R for the given individual. This relation is defined in the following manner. XRY means that the individual in question does not prefer X to Y. Our proposition can be reformulated in terms of mathematical logic. From the two propositions ARB and BRC, ARC follows. The relation R is transitive. Now we use the functional calculus. Let $U(X)$ be the satisfaction or utility of the individual derived from the combination of goods and services X. Then we deduce that if $U(A) \leqq U(B)$ and also $U(B) \leqq U(C)$, it follows that $U(A) \leqq U(C)$. Following Pareto (1927), it can also be shown that utility or satisfaction need not be measurable. An ordinal scale of utility is sufficient. It is easy to see that the three formulations given above are logically equivalent. Hence, non-mathematical economic theoreticians have no reason to reject the last two formulations if they are willing to accept the first.

This short discussion is not presented as a very realistic model of economic choice. It neglects the possibility that utility might be a multidimensional concept (Georgescu-Roegen 1954). This question is discussed below. Also, it neglects the possibility of the existence of a psychological threshold, which might invalidate the transitivity of the concept of indifference (Georgescu-Roegen 1950). For instance, an individual may say he is indifferent between X and Y and also between Y and Z. But still, when confronted by a choice between X and Z, he may prefer Z because of existing psychological thresholds. The problem of measurability in economics has been recently discussed in a most penetrating analysis by Georgescu-Roegen (1965), who especially shows its importance in the theory of production.

Much of the modern discussion of the pure theory of choice is carried on in terms of revealed preference. This is a strictly behavioristic point of view in choice theory, in which we try to discover the underlying structure of choice of a given individual from his overt actions of choice. (Samuelson 1938, 1947, 1948; Houthakker 1950). This point of view has been criticized by Georgescu-Roegen (1950), who has pointed out that the existence of psyschological thresholds may make the recognition of revealed preference (e.g., transitivity of choice) impossible.

Thanks to a method proposed by Wald (1940), we are able to approximate the static utility function or indifference system. By a utility function we mean a function which measures utility or satisfaction derived from various goods and services consumed. An indifference surface indicates combinations of various goods and services which are such that they give the same utility or satisfaction. These ideas are important in the modern theory of demand, because they enable us to explain consistently the quantity demanded of a given commodity or service as a function of the given prices of all commodities and services and of money income. Wald uses quadratic utility functions as approximations. An Engel curve is a relationship between the quantity of a commodity or service consumed and money income, assuming prices being constant. The Engel curves — relations between consumption of a given commodity by an individual and money income of the same individual with constant prices — are linear if the utility function is quadratic. J. A. Nordin (Tintner 1952, pp. 60 ff.) uses data from statistics in the United States 1935–6 and 1941. His first sample includes 300,000 families; his last 3,060. In this highly aggregated model, x is an index of consumption of food and y an index of consumption of non-food — all other items. It is assumed that tastes and preferences of American families have been approximately constant during the period involved; utility is taken as a one-dimensional concept. There is also no consideration of stochastic problems, and the existence of a psychological threshold is ignored. Further, no attention is paid to saving and other dynamic factors which might influence consumption. Finally, there is no consideration of the possible interrelationship of the demand for a given good between individual consumers (Tintner 1946, 1960*b*).

The utility function derived here is an average utility function for the United States. The sample surveys give us numerical information about expenditure on various items — for example, expenditures on food. By dividing food expenditures by an index of food prices, we derive an index of the quantity of food consumed. We also have information about expenditure on all other items. Dividing these expenditure figures by an index of all other prices except food, we derive an index of consumption of non-food.

Let x be consumption of food and y be consumption of all other commodities and services. As an empirical approximation, the following utility function for the American economy is

$$U = -0.000890x^2 + 0.022401xy + 0.008353y^2$$
$$+ 104.572144x + 96.68771y. \tag{2}$$

This utility function is supposed to represent approximately the average American's satisfaction derived and choice between food and all other commodities. Making $U = k$, where k is a constant, we might derive the indifference curves, which show combinations of x (food consumed) and y (all other things consumed) between which the typical American individual is indifferent. Naturally, these indifference curves are only crude approximations and subject to the limitations of the analysis pointed out above. At best, they might give us some idea of the behavior of consumers in the region covered by the data. It is known from the modern theory of indifference curves that we might substitute for this utility function U a non-decreasing function of U: thus

$$V = f(U) \tag{3}$$

as long as

$$dV/dU > 0. \tag{4}$$

This fact emphasizes the ordinal character of the utility function. This example, based by necessity upon an extremely aggregated model, should be interpreted with care. It shows that the "classical" concept of static utility theory can be implemented or at least illustrated by the use of empirical data. The idea of utility is not completely empty, nor does it have to rely on the dubious merits of "introspection" alone. The demand function for food shows the relationship between the quantity of food demanded as a function of the price of food, the price of all other goods, and money income. The demand function for non-food shows the relationship between the quantity of all items other than food consumed as a function of a price index of food, a price index for all other commodities, and money income. The utility function may be used, for example, for the computation of demand functions (see Tintner 1952, p. 61), and these might potentially be useful in policy. The derived functions make it possible also to test indirectly the goodness of approximation of the underlying estimations (for a related method see Afriat 1967).

It should, however, be mentioned that according to Georgescu-Roegen (1954) the very existence of indifference surfaces might be doubted. Following Aristotle and some ideas of the early Austrian writers, this implies the existence of a hierarchy of wants. The more urgent wants will be satisfied first, and less urgent wants only after the satisfaction of the most urgent ones. Georgescu-Roegen (1954) considers as an example the choice between butter and margarine. First, the desire for food (calories) will be fulfilled, then the desire of taste, finally the desire for entertainment. These three form a hierarchical order for choice and give rise to a lexicographical ordering.

One of the most interesting developments of recent years is the theory of *measurable* utility by von Neumann and Morgenstern (1944). The concept of utility has a long history which cannot be presented here (Stigler 1950). It might only be mentioned that Bernouilli (1730) investigated a specific form of measurable utility, characteristically in connection with a problem in probability theory (K. Menger 1934a). The three founders of modern utility theory — C. Menger, Walras, and Jevons — also considered utility measurable. Since Pareto (1927), however, it is recognized that measurable utility is not necessary for the purposes of static economics in order to explain choice in consumption.

TABLE 2

MARSCHAK'S PRESENTATION OF INDIVIDUAL CHOICE
AND RESULTANT CONSEQUENCE

	CONSEQUENCE	
ACTS	State of World (s_1)	State of World (s_2)
a_1.	b	b
a_2.	a	c

Marschak's (1964) concept of individual choice and resultant consequence utilizes some of the ideas of Ramsey (1928) and Savage (1954). Consider an individual who has the choice between two acts a_1 and a_2 and who is faced with two possible states of the world s_1 and s_2. Table 2 shows the choices open to him. If the state of the world is s_1, the consequence of his action will be b if he chooses a_1 and a if he chooses a_2. If the state of the world is s_2, his action a_1 will have consequence b and action a_2 will result in consequence c. There is complete uncertainty about the state of the world. Assume that a is preferred to b and b to c. Let $u(x)$ be the utility of x. To fix an arbitrary scale of utility, we assume that

$$u(c) = 0 \text{ and } u(a) = 1, \tag{5}$$

and it follows that

$$0 \leq u(b) \leq 1. \tag{6}$$

Now assume that the individual has a subjective probability p for the state of the world s_1 and the subjective probability $1-p$ for the state s_2 $(0 \leq p \leq 1)$. We assume that the individual evaluates his actions by the principle of the mathematical expectation of utility. The mathematical expectation is the weighted arithmetic mean with the probabilities as weights. We have for action a_2 the mathematical expectation of utility

$$u(a_2) = u(a)p + u(c) \ (1-p) = p; \qquad (7)$$

and similarly, for action a_1 the mathematical expectation of utility

$$u(a_1) = u(b)p + u(b) \ (1-p) = u(b). \qquad (8)$$

There should be a subjective probability p_0 for the individual at which he is *indifferent* between actions a_1 and a_2. Thus the utility of b is p_0.

$$u(c) = 0 \, u(b) = p_0 \, u(a) = 1. \qquad (9)$$

Hence we have now assigned measurable utility to $a, b,$ and c. These utilities are unique up to a linear transformation. The zero point and the scale of utility can be assigned arbitrarily.

The above example shows how we may construct a measurable utility function, which is determinate except for origin and scale. Any linear function $V = a + bU$ with a and b constant and b positive is equivalent. This example shows also the importance of the axiom of expected utility maximization and the relation between measurable utility and subjective probability.

An interesting theory of utility which tries to explain gambling and the buying of insurance has been proposed by Friedman and Savage (1948). For experimental determination of measurable utility, see Mosteller and Nogee (1951) and Davidson, Siegel, and Suppes (1957). The whole theory has been criticized by Allais (1953) from the point of view of the psychological assumption involved. The von Neumann-Morgenstern concept of measurable utility has been criticized, because utility of gambling and love of danger are excluded (Graff 1957, p. 36; Marschak 1950). This is in many ways a serious shortcoming but may be remedied in time. Nevertheless, the idea of measurable utility represents a great advance in economics and has been used extensively in modern statistics, especially in decision theory (Wald 1950; Blackwell and Girshick 1954) and the personal, subjective, or Bayesian approach to statistics (Savage 1954, 1962).

Statics

Economic statics is defined by Hicks (1946) as the theory of an economic system in which time does not enter, where the variables (prices, quantities produced and consumed, and so on) are not dated. Much of present-day economics is still statics, especially the great system of static equilibrium of Walras. This is perhaps one of the main weaknesses of present-day economics.

One of the most important uses of economic statics is the comparison of two distinct static systems. This is called comparative statics. It has the advantage that frequently important economic conclusions can be derived from very simple assumptions (Samuelson 1947). As an example of comparative statics, consider the position of a simple monopolist in face of a tax (Samuelson 1947, pp. 15–16). Monopoly exists if in a market there is one seller and many buyers. Let x be the output of the monopolist, $f(x)$ the profits before the tax — that is, the difference between total revenue (price times quantity demanded) and total production cost — and t the (constant) tax rate per unit. Hence, we have for the profit after tax

$$P = f(x) - tx. \tag{10}$$

This is maximized if

$$dP/dx = f'(x) - t = 0 \tag{11}$$

and

$$d^2P/dx^2 = f''(x) < 0. \tag{12}$$

We assume that the function $f(x)$ has first and second derivates, denoted by $f'(x)$ and $f''(x)$. To investigate the influence of the tax, we differentiate (11) with respect to the parameter t and obtain

$$f''(x)\ (dx/dt) - 1 = 0. \tag{13}$$

Hence,

$$dx/dt = 1/f''(x) < 0 \tag{14}$$

because of (12). Output will decline with increase of the tax rate t.

As Kaufmann (1944, pp. 218 ff.) points out, to determine the monopoly price and optimum level of output, the monopolist must know (a) his total cost function, (b) the demand function for the product, and (c) the maximum value of the profit function. This might require perfect foresight. Whereas (a) and (b) are synthetic (empirical) propositions, (c) is analytic. These assumptions show that conclusions drawn from comparative statics are frequently of limited validity in practical applications. Nevertheless, since they are relatively easy to obtain from rather simple models, such methods are popular among economists, who do not always realize the severe limitations of the conclusions and do not hesitate to apply the results sometimes to concrete questions of policy.

As an example of the more modern linear methods used in mathematical economics and operations research, let us present a simple instance of linear programing, a method discovered by Kantorovich (1939, 1963) and Dantzig (1949, 1963). Mathematically, the problem of linear programing consists in maximizing (or minimizing) a linear form, subject to linear inequalities and the condition that the solutions might not be negative (Vajda 1961).

Consider the situation of a typical farm in Hancock County, Iowa, during the period 1928–52 (Tintner 1960a). There are two products: corn (x_1) and flax (x_2). We analyze the situation in the short run (Heady and Candler 1958); hence, we can neglect fixed costs — that is, costs which are independent of the amounts produced, since in the short run they are incurred anyway (Tintner 1960a). We consider production in the short run — that is, in a situation where the amount of various factors of production (land, labor, capital) is fixed. Consider land, for instance. In the short run the amount of land is given for the farmer, but he does not have to use his total amount of land and can leave part of it uncultivated. In the long run he may sell some of his land or buy more land. Similar considerations also hold for other factors of production.

Further, we assume constant coefficients of production. This means that the amount of any product (e.g., corn) is proportional to the inputs used in the production of this commodity (proportional to the amounts of land and capital). This assumption must be considered as a great simplification of the real conditions of production. In the short run the amounts of the factors of production used cannot be increased. Also we assume that the farm produces under static conditions. The price of a bushel of corn is \$1.56 and that of a bushel of flax is \$3.81. The "objective function" — the short run profits the farmer wants to maximize — is

$$f = 1.56x_1 + 3.81x_2. \tag{15}$$

For the conditions of production in the short run we again make the simplest possible assumptions — fixed coefficients of production. We assume that outputs are approximately proportional to inputs. The sample survey tells us that it takes an average of 0.022740 acres of land to produce a bushel of corn and an average of 0.09244 acres of land to produce a bushel of flax. The typical farm we are investigating has 148 acres of land. Similarly, it takes an average \$0.317720 of capital to produce a bushel of corn, and on the average of \$0.969500 of capital to produce a bushel of flax. The average capital available for the farm is \$1,800.

Again for the sake of simplicity, we neglect other factors of production apart from land and capital — for example, labor. Now in the short run the farmer can use only the land (148 acres) and the capital (\$1,800) he actually has available. But he is not obliged to utilize all the land and capital he has. In the long run, however, he might sell some land or borrow more capital. The conditions of production in our simple example are in the short run

$$0.022740x_1 + 0.092440x_2 \leqq 148 \qquad (16)$$

and

$$0.317720x_1 + 0.969500x_2 \leqq 1800.$$

To these conditions of production in the short run we must also add the condition that it is impossible to produce negative amounts of corn and flax

$$x_1 \geqq 0, \ x_2 \geqq 0. \qquad (17)$$

The solution to the problem of finding the maximum of short term profits (15) under the stated conditions of short term production may be found by the simplex method of Dantzig (1951, 1963). The results are: To maximize profits the farmer ought to produce $x_1 = 5{,}365.366$ bushels of corn and $x_2 = 0$ bushels of flax. Then his optimal profit will be $f = \$8{,}837.971$. This maximum is achieved if the farmer uses all his available capital ($\$1{,}800$) but only 128.83 acres of the total available 148 acres of land. It is a remarkable mathematical fact that to each maximum problem in linear programming there exists a dual minimum problem. This establishes the formal relation between linear programming and the von Neumann and Morgenstern (1944) theory of two person zero sum games. This dual also has a very interesting economic interpretation.

Again considering our example, the farmer in question will have to establish certain accounting (book keeping) or shadow prices for the two factors of production used. Let u_1 be the shadow price for an acre of land and u_2 the shadow price for each dollar of capital. It should be emphasized that these are merely accounting or shadow prices. They express the rational valuation of units of factors of production (land and capital) for the farmer in the short run and are not necessarily identical with market prices.

Since the typical farm possesses in the short run 148 acres of land and $1,800 of capital, the farmer will try to *minimize*:

$$g = 148u_1 + 1,800u_2 \qquad (18)$$

This expression under our assumptions is the book keeping or accounting cost of the farm enterprise in the short run.

The inequalities imposed are that for each activity (bushels of corn and flax produced) the *imputed cost* (using the accounting prices) must be at least as great as the net price of the activity (price of a bushel of corn or flax): thus

$$0.022740u_1 + 0.317720u_2 \geqq 1.56 \qquad (19)$$

and

$$0.092440u_1 + 0.969500u_2 \geqq 3.81.$$

The last condition says that the accounting prices are not negative:

$$u_1 \geqq 0, \ u_2 \geqq 0. \qquad (20)$$

The solution of this minimum problem is that the imputed price of land is $u_1 = 0$. Land is for the farmer in question a free good, like air. This is shown by the fact that he did not use all the land available (148 acres) but only 128.83 acres. Hence, it would not cost him anything to use more land. The high imputed price of capital, $u_2 = 4.91$, is explained by the scarcity of capital. The total imputed cost $g = \$8,837.971$. Hence, we see that the dual minimum problem has the same solution (minimum value of imputed cost) as the original maximum problem (maximum of short run profits). If the factors of production are correctly evaluated then they exhaust the profits, and no extra profits are made in equilibrium.

In evaluating this example, the following fundamental assumptions used should be kept in mind: The model is static, but the data for its verification are taken from a dynamic economy. We assume pure and perfect competition; that is, the farmer cannot in any way influence the prices at which he sells his products. We investigate production in the short run; that is, the farmer cannot increase or decrease the amounts of the factors of production (land and capital) available to him. Also, for the sake of simplicity we distinguish only two factors of production. In a more realistic investigation labor should be introduced and various types of labor, capital, and land distinguished. The assumption of constant coefficients of production is a very strong one. The output of a given commodity (corn or flax) is strictly proportional to the inputs (land and capital). This is perhaps the most convenient available economic model of production but a great simplification of reality. Finally, we assume that the farmer only tries to maximize his short run profit or equivalently tries to minimize his accounting cost in the short run.

In spite of these severe limitations, the method of linear programming has been applied with some success to concrete economic problems. It should be pointed out that certain generalizations are possible. We might generalize the method by non-linear programming in which neither the objective function nor the inequalities need to be linear (Kuhn and Tucker 1951). When it is necessary for the solutions to be integers (Baumol 1961, pp. 148 ff.), we must use the method of integer programming. The method can also be generalized to deal with dynamic problems — that is, production over time, which leads to dynamic programming (Bellman 1957). Finally, we may introduce probability considerations into a linear program. The methods of stochastic programming will be discussed below (Charnes and Cooper 1959; Moeseke 1965).

One of the most interesting developments in mathematical economics was the introduction of game theory by von Neumann and Morgenstern (1944). Here for the first time we find a mathematical model which is not borrowed from the models of classical (deterministic) physics but from the theory of games of strategy (see also Luce and Raiffa 1957). Games of chance (e.g., roulette, dice) have played a very important part in the development of the theory of probability. But the theory of games is entirely different and has actually very little to do

TABLE 3

GAIN MATRIX OF A (LOSS MATRIX OF B) IN A TWO PERSON ZERO SUM GAME

STRATEGIES OF A	STRATEGIES OF B			ROW MINIMA
	B_1	B_2	B_3	
A_1	21	11	31	11
A_2	32	0	4	0
COLUMN MAXIMA.	32	11	31	

with games of chance (e.g., throwing dice, roulette). It treats, on the contrary, games of strategy (e.g., poker, bridge, or chess) where each participant pursues his aim intelligently. Chance plays a very minor part in this theory, but it is not entirely absent (as in chance moves). Consider a simple example of a two person zero sum game (Tintner 1957). There are two players, A and B. Assume that A plays against B. What A wins B loses, and vice versa (zero sum). The totality of all possible moves of the game by A is called a strategy. Strategies are defined by von Neumann and Morgenstern (1944, p. 79) as follows:

Imagine now that each player . . . instead of making each decision as the necessity for it arises, makes up his mind in advance for all possible contingencies; i.e. that the player . . . begins to play with a complete plan: a plan which specifies what choices he will make in every possible situation, for every possible actual information which he may possess at that moment in conformity with the pattern of information which the rules of the game provide for him in that case. We call such a plan a *strategy.*

Assume that A has the strategies A_1, A_2 and B the strategies B_1, B_2, B_3. In Table 3 it can be seen that the gains of A are at the same time the losses of B. If A uses his strategy A_1, he will gain 21, 11, or 31 according to whether B uses B_1, B_2, or B_3. Since A knows that B is an intelligent opponent and that A's gains are B's losses, B will minimize his loss (which is A's gain). Hence A can only count on winning the *minimum* of the first row, 11, if he uses his strategy A_1. Suppose A uses his strategy A_2. Then, if B uses B_1, B_2, or B_3, he will gain 32, 0, or 4. For the same reasons as before, he can only count on the minimum of the second row, 0.

From the point of view of B the table represents losses. Suppose he uses his strategy B_1. Then, according to whether A uses A_1 or A_2, B may count on a loss of 21 or 32. But since B's loss is A's gain, he can only expect the *maximum* loss, 32, if he uses B_1. Similarly, for his remaining strategies B_2 and B_3 he has to take account of the fact that he must expect for each strategy the maximum loss — 11 for B_2 and 31 for B_3.

An equilibrium exists if the desire of A to maximize his minimum gain for each strategy coincides with the aim of B to minimize his maximum loss for each of his own strategies. This

TABLE 4

GAIN MATRIX OF A (LOSS MATRIX OF B) IN A TWO PERSON ZERO SUM GAME
WITHOUT MINIMAX

STRATEGIES OF A	STRATEGIES OF B			ROW MINIMA
	B_1	B_2	B_3	
A_1	9	10	11	9
A_2	11	10	9	9
A_3	12	10	8	8
COLUMN MAXIMA	12	10	11	

equilibrium solution is a minimax or saddle point. In our simple example it is evidently 11. Hence, A will use A_1, and B will utilize B_2. This combination of strategies make sure that A will gain at least 11, and B will not lose more than 11.

Since the gain and loss matrix is arbitrary, we might well ask if there is always an equilibrium. It is of course easy to construct matrices which have no minimax. Consider, for instance, a case where A and B have 3 strategies (Table 4). It is evident that in this case no minimax exists. But if we change the problem slightly, we may consider the situation where A and B play the game not just once but many times. Suppose that A uses the strategy A_1 with a probability p_1, the strategy A_2 with probability p_2, and A_3 with probability p_3. Also, B uses strategy B_1 with probability q_1, B_2 with probability q_2, and B_3 with probability q_3. In a long series of games played by A and B the average gain of A (loss of B) will be the mathematical expectation

E, which is the weighted arithmetic mean of the gains or losses with the probabilities as weights. Thus,

$$E = 9p_1q_1 + 10p_1q_2 + 11p_1q_3 + 11p_2q_1 + 10p_2q_2 + 9p_2q_3$$
$$+ 12p_3q_1 + 10p_3q_2 + 8p_3q_3. \tag{21}$$

Assume that A tries to maximize and B tries to minimize the mathematical expectation (21). Then A has the choice of two probability distributions: $p_1 = 2/3$, $p_2 = 0$, $p_3 = 1/3$; and alternatively, $p_1 = 1/2$, $p_2 = 1/2$, $p_3 = 0$. B has to choose the probability distribution: $q_1 = 0$, $q_2 = 1$, $q_3 = 0$, or $q_1 = \frac{1}{2}$, $q_1 = 0$ $q_3 = \frac{1}{2}$. If A and B choose their strategies with the indicated probabilities, the mathematical expectation of the gain of A (loss of B) is $E = 10$ — this is to say that by choosing the given probabilities, A can make sure to gain at least 10 in a long series of games, and B can make sure to lose not more than 10 in a long series.

Ideas based on the theory of games have been very important in modern mathematical economics in connection with the theory of measurable utility, decision theory, and the theory of static general equilibrium systems under free competition. The theory has not yet been quite successful in connection with problems of market organization, which are in a sense between free competition (many buyers and sellers) and monopoly (one seller) or monopsony (one buyer) (Shubik 1959). The problem of market organizations which are neither purely competitive (a great number of buyers and sellers) nor monopoly (one seller) nor monopsony (one buyer) has stubbornly resisted theoretical analysis. These are problems of oligopoly (a few sellers), oligopsony (a few buyers), bilateral monopoly (one seller and one buyer), and so on. Game theory has made a valuable contribution by pointing out that the main problem is the formation of *coalitions* (Shubik 1959).

We shall discuss a bargaining model, using bilateral monopoly (one seller, one buyer) as an example. The problem of bilateral monopoly is very important in the labor market, where, for example, a labor union faces a single monopolistic enter-

prise or a cartelized or trustified industry. An interesting bar-
ing model has been proposed by Harsanyi (1962) on the basis
of a theory by Nash (1953), which has its origin in Zeuthen's ideas (1933). Assume that two people bargain, whose
utility we denote by u_1 and u_2. We define a prospect space, the
set of all utilities the two bargainers can obtain by a joint
strategy. Let the conflict point C represent the utility they would
obtain if they could not reach agreement. Then a maximization
of the product,

$$[u_1(S) - u_1(C)] \cdot [u_2(S) - u_2(C)], \qquad (22)$$

with respect to S over the whole prospect space will determine
the solution. As Harsanyi (1962, p. 449) points out, this solution of the bargaining problem gives intuitively attractive results:

In general, the Nash solution assigns to any party a larger payoff: 1. the
larger the party's willingness to risk a conflict rather than making conces-
sions to his opponent. 2. the smaller the other party's willingness to risk
a conflict. 3. the larger the damage that in the case of a conflict the first
party could cause to the second party, at a given cost to himself. 4. the
smaller the damage that the second party could cause to the first party at
a given cost to himself. (See also Harsanyi 1966.)

The following discussion of the existence and uniqueness of
the Walras-Cassel system of competitive static equilibrium is
an adaptation of an earlier discussion by Wald (1951) and by
Dorfmann, Samuelson, and Solow (1958, p. 346 ff.). A more
detailed investigation is found in Debreu (1959).

We assume constant coefficients of production: a_{ij} is the
amount of factor i used in producing the commodity j. Let
$x_1, x_2, \ldots, x_n$ be the amounts of the n commodities produced,
$r_1, r_2, \ldots, r_m$ the amounts of the m resources or factors of
production utilized. The total amount of factor i used in the production of commodity j is then $a_{ij}x_j$. The total amount of
the factor i used in the production of all commodities in the
economy is $a_{i1}x_1 + a_{i2}x_2 + \ldots + a_{in}x_n$. But evidently this can-

35

not be greater than the total amount of the factor i available, r_i. Hence we obtain the system of inequalities

$$a_{11}x_1 + a_{12}x_2 + \ldots + a_{1n}x_n \leqq r_1 \qquad (23)$$

$$a_{21}x_1 + a_{22}x_2 + \ldots + a_{2n}x_n \leqq r_2$$

$$\ldots \ldots \ldots \ldots \ldots \ldots \ldots \ldots \ldots$$

$$a_{m1}x_1 + a_{m2}x_2 + \ldots + a_{mn}x_n \leqq r_m.$$

Inequalities are introduced because some of the resources might be redundant and then become free goods (i.e., their prices are zero).

Let $p_1, p_2, \ldots, p_n$ be the prices of the n final goods and $v_1, v_2, \ldots, v_m$ be the prices of the m factors of production. We assume that there are market demand equations for all final commodities, which (in principle) depend on all the prices

$$x_1 = F_1 (p_1, p_2, \ldots, p_n, v_1, v_2, \ldots, v_m) \qquad (24)$$

$$x_2 = F_2 (p_1, p_2, \ldots, p_n, v_1, v_2, \ldots, v_m)$$

$$\ldots \ldots \ldots \ldots \ldots \ldots \ldots \ldots$$

$$x_n = F_n (p_1, p_2, \ldots, p_n, v_1, v_2, \ldots, v_m).$$

These demand functions are homogeneous of degree zero in the prices; that is, if *all* prices are multiplied by a positive constant L, the quantities demanded are not changed:

$$F_i (Lp_1, Lp_2, \ldots, Lp_n, Lv_1, Lv_2, \ldots, Lv_m)$$
$$= F_i (p_1, p_2, \ldots, p_n, v_1, v_2, \ldots, v_m).$$

The supply functions of the factors of production are

$$r_1 = G_1 (p_1, p_2, \ldots, p_n, v_1, v_2, \ldots, v_m) \qquad (26)$$

$$r_2 = G_2 (p_1, p_2, \ldots, p_n, v_1, v^2, \ldots, v_m)$$

$$\ldots \ldots \ldots \ldots \ldots \ldots \ldots \ldots \ldots$$

$$r_m = G_m (p_1, p_2, \ldots, p_n, v_1, v_2, \ldots, v_m).$$

These functions are also homogeneous of degree zero in the prices. If *all* prices are multiplied by the same positive constant, the quantities supplied are not changed.

The cost of factor i in the production of commodity j is $a_{ij}v_i$. The total cost per unit of producing commodity j is under our assumptions $a_{1j}v_1 + a_{2j}v_2 + \ldots + a_{mj}v_m$. But this unit cost cannot be smaller than the price of the commodity p_j. In long run static competitive equilibrium the price of each commodity cannot be greater than the unit costs:

$$a_{11}v_1 + a_{21}v_2 + \ldots + a_{m1}v_m \geqq p_1 \qquad (27)$$

$$a_{12}v_1 + a_{22}v_2 + \ldots + a_{m2}v_m \geqq p_2$$

$$\ldots \ldots \ldots \ldots \ldots \ldots \ldots \ldots \ldots \ldots \ldots \ldots \ldots \ldots \ldots$$

$$a_{1n}v_1 + a_{2n}v_2 + \ldots + a_{mn}v_m \geqq p_n.$$

If the strict inequality sign holds in any of the equations, then the unit cost of producing this commodity is greater than its price, and the corresponding output of the commodity in question is zero. If the cost of production is greater than the price of a commodity, the commodity is not produced.

By methods related to linear programming, the existence of a system of solutions for the quantities of the final commodities $x_1, x_2, \ldots, x_n$, their prices $p_1, p_2, \ldots, p_n$, the quantities $r_1, r_2, \ldots, r_m$, and the prices of the factors of production $v_1, v_2, \ldots, v_m$ can be proved; and these results are economically meaningful since none of these quantities is negative. If some rather strong assumptions are also made about the demand functions, it can be shown that the solutions are unique.

For the sake of simplicity this model of general static competitive economic equilibrium has been presented in a highly aggregative form. It can be shown, however, that individual demand functions for all commodities and individual supply functions of original services (labor) for all individuals in the system can be determined from the modern theory of choice. Similarly, the theory of production can be used to find the demand for all factors of production and the supply of all final products by competitive firms (Hicks 1946). Under our assumptions of atomistic independence it would then be possible to simply add these individual demand and supply functions, which form the basis of the system actually investigated. Morgenstern (1947) has pointed out that this procedure is not permissible if we deviate from our assumptions.

Competition has been defined by Moore (1929) as involving the following principles: every economic factor seeks and obtains a maximum net income; there is but one price of the commodities of the same quality in the same market; the influence of the product of any one producer upon the price per unit of the total product is negligible; the output of any one producer is negligible as compared with the total output; each producer regulates the amount of his output without regard to the effects of his act upon the conduct of his competitors. These conditions should warn us that the application of the model described above to a concrete economic system would be very hazardous.

There has been a great deal of discussion of the stability of solutions of a static competitive economic system. The discussion has been conveniently summarized by Morishima (1964); but since the assumptions of the theory are unrealistic, it seems to be only remotely connected with a truly dynamic theory of economics.

It might be mentioned that several authors (Koopmans 1957; Debreu 1959; Malinvaud 1953; Kuenne 1963) have extended this model in a number of directions to include individual households and consumption, and also individual competitive firms. The model could be generalized to include production and consumption over time and even certain aspects of uncertainty (Arrow and Debreu 1959). We should in all honesty, however, remember some of the fundamental restrictions which cannot be removed: All commodities and services are indefinitely divisible, and the problem of indivisibilities has, up to now, resisted analysis (Lerner 1944; Koopmans and Beckman 1957; Hurwicz 1960). Also, no elements of monopoly and similar phenomena can be included.

As a small example of the empirical analysis of a static system, I would like to present a model of the Portuguese economy in the year 1957 (Tintner and Murteira 1960; Tintner 1965). This economy is divided into 4 sectors: (1) all enterprises; (2) government; (3) foreign trade; (4) households. Such a highly aggregated system, of course, is not very useful, but Leontief (1951) and others have calculated systems with many more sectors. With data taken from national accounting in Portugal, we can compute the constant coefficients of production. The assumption is that in a first approximation the Portuguese economy works under conditions of constant coefficients of production — that is to say, we assume that the output of each sector is strictly proportional to the inputs coming from other sectors. We also assume perfect competition.

Let X_1 be the net output of the enterprise sector, X_2 the value of government services, and X_3 the value of exports. The net output of each sector is the output absorbed by the other sectors. Designate the demand of private consumers for products of the enterprise sector by y_1, the demand of consumers for government services by y_2, and their demand for imports by y_3. The demand of the private consumers is assumed to be given.

With our assumptions we derive the following system:

$$X_1 = 1.276y_1 + 0.635y_2 + 1.000y_3 \qquad (28)$$
$$X_2 = 0.084y_1 + 1.042y_2 + 0.184y_3$$
$$X_3 = 0.323y_1 + 0.161y_2 + 1.253y_3.$$

This system shows the linear dependence of the net output of each sector (X_1, X_2, X_3) upon the autonomous demand of consumers in Portugal for the goods and services of the three sectors (y_1, y_2, y_3).

The interpretation of these results is as follows: Assume that our hypotheses (constant coefficients of production and free competition) hold, at least approximately, in the Portuguese economy. Assume further that the demand for products and services of the enterprise sector (y_1) alone increases by 1 escudo.

We may then expect that the net product of the enterprise sector will increase by 1.276 escudos, the net value of government services by 0.084 escudos, the value of exports by 0.323 escudos. Assume now that *ceteris paribus* the demand of households for government services (y_2) increases by 1 escudo. The effects on the net output of the various sectors is as follows: The net output of enterprises must increase by 0.635 escudos, the value of government services by 1.042 escudos, the value of exports by 0.161 escudos. Finally, if *ceteris paribus* the demand of households for imports (y_3) increases by 1 escudo, the effects are as follows: We might expect the net product of enterprises to increase by 1 escudo, the value of government services to increase by 0.184 escudos, the value of exports by 1.253 escudos.

This analysis of the Portuguese economy should be considered only as an example which demonstrates the general methodology of input-output analysis. For a serious investigation of a given economic system the economy must of course be divided into many sectors. Apart from this great simplification, there are certain other hypotheses which underlie the analysis: We assume constant coefficients of production: that is, in each sector outputs are strictly proportional to inputs. Also, free and perfect competition is assumed. Capital and stocks are here neglected. No attention is paid to monetary phenomena. The final demand of the families for the goods and services of the various sectors is assumed to be given. It should perhaps be pointed out that all these assumptions are not very realistic for the Portuguese economy. Systems of this kind are called input-output systems (Leontief systems). They are of course more useful if they contain more sectors than our small model. They can also be generalized to include capital and other phenomena (Leontief 1951; Dorfman, Samuelson, and Solow 1958) and they play a certain role in the theoretical analysis of dynamic phenomena (Morishima 1964). The development of input-output systems (Leontief 1951), which has been exemplified above, belongs to the most successful and interesting advances of econometrics. Many such empirical systems with a great many sectors have been constructed in various countries (Chenery and Clark 1959). They are very useful for short term prediction and may also be combined with other econometric models, which are not necessarily linear, for the study of a national economy like the recent extensive model of the United States (Duesenberry *et al* 1966).

Non-Static Systems

The philosopher Northrop (1947, p. 235) makes an important contribution with his greatly detailed examination of what he calls "classical economic science." He comes to the conclusion that on this basis no economic dynamics is possible. This conclusion is certainly justified insofar as the systems investigated are by their very assumption static. In order to make them dynamic (i.e., in order to introduce time) special additional assumptions are needed, which are mostly concerned with the theory of anticipation of relevant economic quantities (Hicks 1946; Tintner 1942*a-c*, 1941) — for example, anticipated prices (G. G. Granger 1955, p. 88 ff., 1960).

All economic phenomena which are not static we call non-static. Following the ideas of Knight (1933), non-static economic phenomena are classified as follows: dynamics — single valued anticipations; risk — existence of a single known probability distribution of anticipations; uncertainty — existence of several probability distributions of anticipations, perhaps connected by an a priori probability distribution.

In Hicks (1946) view of dynamics anticipations are single valued — that is, we assume that faced with a decision about present behavior which involves the future, the individual households and firms have unique and single valued anticipations (Tintner 1941, 1942*a-c*). This is, of course, only a limiting case. Consider a farmer who has to plan his crop. He must take into account the anticipated future price of the commodity he produces at the time when the production will be finished.

As an example, consider an empirical investigation of the production of pork in Austria, 1948–55 (Tintner 1960*c*, p. 85). Denote the logarithm of the quantity of pork offered in the year

t by X_{1t} and the logarithm of the price of pork in the year t by X_{2t}. The estimate of the supply function of pork in Austria is

$$X_{1t} = 0.81 + 0.74X_{2t-1}. \tag{29}$$

The assumption here is that the anticipated price of pork is equal to the existing price of pork at the time of the start of production. This equation gives us an estimate of the elasticity of the supply of pork — namely, 0.74. This has to be interpreted in this way: Assume that the price of pork increases by 1 per cent in a given year. We might then predict an increase of the supply of pork in the next year of about ¾ per cent. Dynamic problems have been studied by many economists and econometricians, especially Roos (1934) and Evans (1930). There are also related studies of business cycle phenomena — for example, Kalecki (1935). In recent years the problem of economic growth has come into the foreground, especially in connection with the underdeveloped countries (Baumol 1959; Higgins 1959).

Friedman (1957) has computed a "dynamic" consumption function for the United States 1905–1951 (war years omitted). Let C_t be consumption and R_t disposable income in the year t. The empirical relation is

$$C_t = 0.58R_t + 0.32R_{t-1} + 53. \tag{30}$$

The short term marginal propensity to consume is 0.58 and the long term marginal propensity is $0.58 + 0.32 = 0.90$ — that is, if disposable income (income received by consumers) increases by \$1.00, in the short run consumption will increase by \$0.58 and in the long run by \$0.90. A more complicated model gives

$$C_t = 0.29R_t + 0.19R_{t-1} + 0.13R_{t-2} \\ + 0.09R_{t-3} + 0.06R_{t-4} + 0.04R_{t-5} + \ldots -4. \tag{31}$$

In this more comprehensive model the short term propensity to consume is 0.29, and the long term propensity is 0.88. This is of course a very highly aggregated model and some of its assumptions must be taken into account: There is no change in the consumption habits of the persons in the economy involved during the period investigated. Consumption depends *only* upon disposable income and anticipated disposable income, which is approximated as a linear function of the disposable income in the past. More complicated and more truly dynamic models which make consumption depend upon the highest experienced income of the past are by Modigliani (1949) and Duesenberry (1949).

It is undeniable that ideas about economic development which have been discussed in the recent past (Harrod 1952; Higgins 1959; Domar 1957; von Neumann 1945) are closely related to concepts of the classical school of economics and of Marx (Lange 1963). This is particularly apparent in the recent book of Morishima (1964, pp. 136 ff.) which introduces Marxist ideas explicitly.

One of the most interesting and most discussed models of economic development is the one proposed by von Neumann (1945). In Morishima's interpretation (1964, pp. 131 ff.) consumption of goods takes place only through the processes of production, which includes necessities of life consumed by the workers. Wages are at the subsistence level, and all capitalist income is reinvested. This model can be illustrated by an example in which only two goods are produced and three processes of production available, although the model was given originally for any number of goods and processes.

Let c_{ij} by the input coefficient of process i for good j. This includes the quantity of good j technologically necessary per unit of process i, and also the minimum of good j necessary to persuade people employed in process i to work. The output coefficient b_{ij} is the quantity of good j produced in process i. The coefficients are assumed to be constants. Each process has unit duration (e.g., one year). Processes of longer duration than one time unit are broken down into a number of processes with unit duration.

Let $f(t)$ be the interest factor in period t, that is, one plus the rate of interest (expressed in decimals). Thus in this notation if the rate of interest is 5 per cent, then $f(t) = 1.05$. Also, $q_1(t)$, $q_2(t)$, $q_3(t)$ are the intensities of the processes of production (e.g., number of bushels of corn produced, etc.). $P_1(t)$ and $P_2(t)$ are the prices of the two commodities. Since competitive equilibrium is assumed, there cannot be any processes which yield a return *greater* than the prevailing rate of interest, because under perfect competition extra profits would attract competitors to use the same process, and the prices of factors of production would rise. Hence symbolically,

$$(32)$$

$$b_{11}P_1(t+1) + b_{12}P_2(t+1) \leqq f(t)\,[c_{11}P_1(t) + c_{12}P_2(t)]$$

and

$$b_{21}P_1(t+1) + b_{22}P_2(t+1) \leqq f(t)\,[c_{21}P_1(t) + c_{22}P_2(t)]$$

and

$$b_{31}P_1(t+1) + b_{32}P_2(t+1) \leqq f(t)\,[c_{31}P_1(t) + c_{32}P_2(t)].$$

The first inequality refers to the first process. It shows that the output of this process evaluated at the prices prevailing at time $t+1$ cannot be greater than the cost of this process, evaluated at the prices at time t and multiplied by the interest factor, $f(t)$. If the inequality sign holds, the process will not be used; then $q_1(t)$ is equal to zero. Similar considerations hold for the second and third commodity. Hence it follows that in equilibrium

$$
\begin{aligned}
q_1(t)b_{11}P_1(t+1) + q_1(t)b_{12}P_2(t+1) \qquad (33) \\
+ q_2(t)b_{21}P_1(t+1) + q_2(t)b_{22}P_2(t+1) \\
+ q_3(t)b_{31}P_1(t+1) + q_3(t)b_{32}P_2(t+1) = \\
f(t)\,[q_1(t)c_{11}P_1(t) + q_1(t)c_{12}P_2(t) + q_2(t)c_{21}P_1(t) + \\
q_2(t)c_{22}P_2(t) + q_3(t)c_{31}P_1(t) + q_3(t)c_{32}P_2(t)].
\end{aligned}
$$

The left hand side shows the total value of the production at time t evaluated with the prices at time $t+1$ when the production process is finished. The right hand side is the total cost of production, evaluated at prices at time t, times the interest factor. These two quantities must be equal for equilibrium.

Since one cannot consume more of a given good than is available from the production of the preceding period, we have the inequalities,

$$q_1(t-1)b_{11} + q_2(t-1)b_{21} + q_3(t-1)b_{31} \geqq \qquad (34)$$
$$q_1(t)c_{11} + q_2(t)c_{21} + q_3(t)c_{31}$$

and

$$q_1(t-1)b_{12} + q_2(t-1)b_{22} + q_3(t-1)b_{32} \geqq$$
$$q_1(t)c_{12} + q_2(t)c_{22} + q_3(t)c_{32}.$$

The first inequality refers to the first commodity. On the left hand side we have the total amount of this good produced at period $t-1$. This must be greater than or equal to the quantity of this good necessary as an input at period t. If the inequality sign actually holds, the good is a free good and its price $P_1(t) = 0$. We argue similarly for the second commodity thus,

$$q_1(t-1)b_{11}P_1(t) + q_1(t-1)b_{12}P_2(t) + q_2(t-1) \quad (35)$$
$$b_{21}P_1(t) + q_2(t-1)b_{22}P_2(t) + q_3(t-1)b_{31}P_1(t) +$$
$$q_3(t-1)b_{32}P_2(t) =$$
$$q_1(t)c_{11}P_1(t) + q_1(t)c_{12}P_2(t) + q_2(t)c_{21}P_1(t) +$$
$$q_2(t)c_{22}P_2(t) + q_3(t)c_{31}P_1(t) + q_3(t)c_{32}P_2(t).$$

This equation tells us that under our assumption of free competition the total value of the output of the economy in period $t-1$ evaluated at prices at period t (left side of the equation) must be exactly equal to the total value of the input necessary at period t (right side of the equation).

We will have *balanced growth* if the prices are constant:

$$P_1(t) = P_1(t+1), \; P_2(t) = P_2(t+1). \qquad (36)$$

If the interest factor is constant,

$$f(t) = c. \qquad (37)$$

45

If intensities of processes in subsequent periods are proportional,

$$q(t) = aq(t-1). \tag{38}$$

Here a is constant, equal to one plus the rate of balanced growth, $a = c$. This implies exponential growth, or growth in a geometric series.

Von Neumann assumed that all the input and output coefficients are non-negative, but he also assumed, rather unrealistically, that every good is involved as input or output in every process. In that case the system yields unique solutions for c and a, and the interest and growth factor are equal. There may be, however, several solutions for the intensities $q_i(t)$ and the prices $P_j(t)$.

In a generalization of the model Kemeny, Morgenstern, and Thompson (1956) make additional assumptions: The total value of all goods produced must be positive, every good can be produced by some processes, and every process uses some inputs. Under these conditions, but without the unrealistic assumption of von Neumann, they are able to prove the existence but not the uniqueness of the growth and interest factors, which are again equal.

The von Neumann model leads to exponential growth — that is, growth in a geometric series. If some further quite restrictive assumptions are made (Morishima 1964, pp. 154 ff.; Radner 1961), then it can be proved that the following holds: If an economy starts from any quite arbitrary situation and wishes to reach a certain final situation, also almost as arbitrary, it will in the long run be best to follow von Neumann — that is, the behavior of the corresponding von Neumann model (turnpike theorem). This theorem, in spite of very restrictive assumptions, is useful for problems connected with the development of underdeveloped countries.

The Ramsey (1928) model in the form given by Stone (1962) illustrates dynamic models in the narrow sense that we present. (See also Allen 1949, pp. 536 ff.) This highly aggregated model assumes the existence of a production function;

$$Y = f(L, K); \qquad (39)$$

where Y is a product in general, L labor, and K capital stock. In this model, like in many more modern models of economic development, we reduce the whole economy to one single sector. All labor utilized is aggregated into an index of total labor used in the economy. Also, the value of all capital goods (factories, machinery, land) used in the economy is represented by a single index of capital goods. Similarly, it is assumed that all consumption goods used by various individuals in the economy can be aggregated into a single index of consumption. The satisfaction enjoyed by consumption will be represented by a single, average utility function: $\partial Y/\partial L$ is the marginal product of labor — that is, the increment in the total product (Y) if labor (L) increases by a small unit. Similarly, $\partial Y/\partial K$ is the marginal product of capital — that is, the increment in total product (Y) resulting if capital stock (K) increases by a small unit. The time derivative of the capital stock $K: I = dK/dt$ is investment. Let C be consumption. Then by definition

$$C = Y - I = Y - dK/dt \qquad (40)$$

Consumption is the difference between total product and investment. Let the utility of consumption be

$$M = h(C). \qquad (41)$$

Utility is assumed to be measurable. The derivative of this function $h'(C)$ is the marginal utility — that is, the additional utility of a small increment of consumption. The disutility of labor is

$$N = g(L). \qquad (42)$$

Again disutility is measurable. The derivative of this function $g'(L)$ is marginal disutility — that is, the incremental disutility of a small increase in labor. Hence, total utility is

$$U = M - N. \tag{43}$$

Total utility is utility of consumption minus disutility of labor. To maximize,

$$W = \int_{t_1}^{t_2} U \, dt. \tag{44}$$

This is the sum (integral) of total utility between t_1 and t_2. By using the methods of the calculus of variations (Allen 1949, pp. 521 ff.) we derive the following results:

$$\partial Y / \partial L = g'(L) / h'(C). \tag{45}$$

At all times the marginal product of labor must equal the ratio of the marginal disutility of labor to the marginal utility of consumption.

$$\partial Y / \partial K = \frac{dh'(C)/dt}{h'(C)} \tag{46}$$

At all times the marginal product of capital must be equal to the proportionate rate of decrease of the marginal utility of consumption over time. This purely theoretical model throws some light on a problem which is of great importance in connection with economic development, especially of underdeveloped countries: What is (in a sense) an optimal allocation between consumption and investment?

By abandoning the somewhat unreal but convenient assumption of single value anticipations, we have a case of *risk* (Tintner 1941, 1942*a-c*). Here we assume not a unique value of anticipated conditions (prices etc.), but probability distributions of anticipations. At least these probability distributions, however, are known.

As an example, consider again the situation of an Iowa farm (Tintner 1960*a*). We assume that the farmer uses only two factors of production, land and capital, since labor is abundant. With data from the period 1938–52, we estimate the probability distribution of the input coefficients of land and capital in the production of corn and flax. We then determine by numerical methods the approximate probability distribution of the short run net profit of the farmer. This is a problem of *stochastic programming*. The input coefficients are assumed to be normally and independently distributed. By numerical methods we may approximate the probability distribution of short term profits (thus in our example the arithmetic mean of profits is $11,081).

TABLE 5

ARITHMETIC MEAN OF PROFITS ACCORDING TO PROPORTIONAL USE
OF *Land* vs. *Capital* FOR CORN AND FLAX
(In Dollars)

PROPORTION OF CAPITAL USED FOR PRODUCTION OF CORN (Rest in Flax)	PROPORTION OF LAND USED FOR PRODUCTION OF CORN (Rest in Flax)		
	None	One-Half	All
None	5,704	5,168	0
One-Half	4,082	7,008	4,945
All	0	5,075	8,472

This is called the *passive* approach. It may be used for comparing, for example, the probability distribution of profits for a farm in Iowa with those of a farm in California.

More important perhaps is the *active* approach in which the decision variables are the proportions of the factors of production (land and capital) assigned to growing various crops (corn and flax). In Table 5 the arithmetic mean of the estimated probability distribution of short term profits for various possible allocations of the factors of production (land and capital) is shown. The entries in this table must be interpreted in the following way: Assume that the farmer uses no land for corn (hence all the land for flax). He also utilizes no capital for corn and all the capital for flax. Then, his average profit in the short run will be $5,704; but if he divides both land and capital evenly between the two commodities corn and flax, he will receive on the average $7,008. It is easily seen from this table that the best policy for the farmer is the following: He should devote all his land and all his capital to corn, none to flax. Then, under our very simplified conditions his average short term profit will be $8,472, which is the highest he can obtain.

We should mention again that of course some very unrealistic assumptions underly our analysis. The probability distribution of our input coefficients is assumed known; actually it is estimated from past experience. Very crude numerical methods have been utilized to estimate the mean values of profits found in the table. The enormous amount of computations involved, even for a simple example, makes this method of stochastic

TABLE 6

DECISIONS UNDER UNCERTAINTY—*Individual* vs. *Nature*

STRATEGIES OF THE INDIVIDUAL (Values of a)	STRATEGIES OF NATURE (Values of x)				ROW MINIMA	ROW MAXIMA
	0	1	2	3		
0	0	0	0	0	0	0
1	—0.75	0.25	0.25	0.25	—0.75	0.25
2	—1.50	—0.50	0.50	0.50	—1.50	0.50
3	—2.25	—1.25	—0.25	0.75	—2.25	0.75
COLUMN MAXIMA. . .	0	0.25	0.50	0.75		

linear programming impractical for the study of important and realistic empirical problems. (See also Sengupta, Tintner, Morrison 1963.)

The case of risk concerns a situation in which the relevant probability distributions are known. This means in practice that we are dealing with a stable situation (unchanging tastes and technology) and that we have ample experience in the past to estimate accurately the relevant probability distributions. If this is not the case, if the underlying probability distributions are not known, we deal with a case of *uncertainty*.

Consider now the general problem of decisions under uncertainty (Tintner 1959, 1966). This is also called "games against nature" (Milnor 1964). We utilize a game theoretical setup and assume that the strategies of nature are $x = 0, 1, 2, 3$ and that the possible strategies of the individual playing against nature are the actions $a = 0, 1, 2, 3$. (See Table 6.) If the individual chooses the action a = 1, he will get − 0.75 if nature plays the strategy x = 0 and 0.25 if nature is in the state x = 1, 2 or 3.

According to the *minimax criterion* of Wald (1950; see also Davidson *et al.* 1957) the individual has to treat nature as if he was playing a two person zero sum game. He has always to expect the worst. This is expressed in our table as the minimum for each row — that is, for each strategy of the individual. It is sensible under such conditions that the individual will maximize the row minimum — that is, choose the largest figure

TABLE 7

Savage's Matrix Applied to Games against Nature

Strategies of the Individual (Values of *a*)	Strategies of Nature (Values of *x*)				Row Minima
	0	1	2	3	
0.	0.00	−0.25	−0.50	−0.75	−0.75
1	−0.75	0.00	−0.25	−0.50	−0.75
2	−1.50	−0.75	0.00	−0.25	−1.50
3	−2.25	−1.50	−0.75	0.00	−2.25

among the row minima. Hence, in our case the individual will choose action a = 0, since this is the maximum of all the figures in the column of row minima. This procedure has been criticized from the point of view of personal subjective probability by Savage (1954, pp. 200 ff.; see also Good 1950).

The *regret* matrix of Savage (1954 pp. 163 ff.) is formed by considering the regret of the acting individual as the loss occurring between the actual result for a given strategy and the result which could be obtained if the state of nature was known. By deducting the column maxima from each figure in its given column of Table 6 we obtain the regret matrix of Savage (see Table 7). By the application of the minimax principle to the regret matrix, the individual will choose the maximum from among the row minima. Thus, in our case, he is free to choose *a* = 0 or *a* = 1.

Another criterion has been given by Hurwicz (Luce and Raifa 1957, pp. 282 ff.). Consider an individual who is influenced by the worst (row minimum) and the best (row maximum) that could happen for each of his strategies. His criterion is a weighted arithmetic mean of the maximum and minimum (see Table 8). The weights chosen may be regarded as measures of the optimism or pessimism of the individual. For instance, if he gives equal weight to the best and worst for each strategy (0.5min + 0.5max), he will choose $a = 0$ as the best strategy. On

TABLE 8

Measure of Individual Optimism or Pessimism

Strategy of the Individual (Value of a)	Row Minimum (Table 6)	Row Maximum (Table 6)	0.5 Minimum + 0.5 Maximum	0.1 Minimum + 0.9 Maximum
0	0.00	0.00	0.00	0.00
1	—0.75	0.25	—0.25	0.15
2	—1.50	0.50	—0.50	0.30
3	—2.25	0.75	—0.75	0.45

TABLE 9

Laplace's Criterion

Strategy of the Individual (Value of a)	Expected Profit
0	0
1	0
2	—0.25
3	—0.75

the other hand, if he is more optimistic and acts according to 0.1min + 0.9max, he will choose $a = 3$.

Another method is Laplace's criterion. Consider all 4 strategies of nature equally probable and compute the mathematical expectation for each strategy (see Table 9). In our example the individual who wants to maximize the expected profit (computed with the help of the Laplace assumption) will have the choice between strategies $a = 0$ and $a = 1$. Other possibilities are the assignment of a priori probabilities with the help of the theory of logical probability of Carnap (1950).

Here I want to show how one version of the probability theory of Carnap might be used in the face of complete uncertainty to construct a decision model. We are dealing with a perishable commodity and also an entirely new commodity where no past experience is possible. Consider for instance a man who contemplates constructing a rocket for commercial travel to the moon (Tintner 1959, 1960d, 1966). This is a simple version of an inventory problem. How big a rocket should he construct?

Assume that there are only two customers, C_1 and C_2. Each

TABLE 10

APPLICATION OF CARNAP'S THEORY OF LOGICAL PROBABILITY
(Number of Tickets)

STATE DESCRIPTION	CUSTOMER'S ACTION		A PRIORI PROBABILITY
	C_1	C_2	
1	0	0	1/6
2	0	1	1/12
3	1	0	1/12
4	0	2	1/12
5	2	0	1/12
6	1	1	1/6
7	1	2	1/12
8	2	1	1/12
9	2	2	1/6

of these might buy 0, 1 or 2 tickets. In this universe Table 10 shows us all that could happen. Each line in this table is a *state description*. In the first line none of the customers buys a ticket. In the second the first customer buys none, but the second buys one. In the third C_1 buys one, and the C_2 buys none. In the fourth the C_1 buys no ticket, but the second customer buys two, and so on.

Now, according to Carnap's theory, we must treat the two individuals on a par. The entrepreneur does not care who buys the tickets but only how many are sold. Hence we see that certain state descriptions may be obtained by permutation of the two individuals. These are the *structure descriptions*, which

TABLE 11

GAIN OF THE ENTREPRENEUR
(In Money Units)

NUMBER OF SEATS SOLD (x)	A PRIORI PROBABILITY (P_x)	GAIN PER NUMBER OF PLACES (Values of a)				
		0	1	2	3	4
0	1/6	0	—1	—2	—3	—4
1	1/6	0	1	0	—1	—2
2	1/3	0	1	2	1	0
3	1/6	0	1	2	3	2
4	1/6	0	1	2	3	4
MATHEMATICAL EXPECTATION		0	2/3	1	2/3	0

are classes of equivalent state descriptions. In table 10, structure descriptions are separated by horizontal lines. Hence, state descriptions 2 and 3 form one structure description, 4 and 5 constitute another structure description, and 7 and 8 still another structure description. State descriptions 1, 6, and 9 each form a structure description. According to one version of Carnap's probability theory (see Table 10) we give each structure description the same a priori probability. Since there are 6 structure descriptions, each receives probability 1/6; within each structure description each state description receives the same probability. The a priori probabilities of the state descriptions are indicated in the last column of the table.

Now assume that it costs 1 money unit to construct one place in the rocket and that each ticket may be sold for 2 money units. Hence, if a rocket of a places is available and x places are sold, the profit is given by

$$P = 2x - a, \quad 0 \leqq x \leqq a, \tag{47}$$

and

$$P = a \quad , \qquad x > a.$$

For various sizes of the rocket (a) and for various numbers of places sold (x) we obtain Table 11.

The a priori probabilities are taken from Table 10. Assume

that $a = 2$ (i.e., a rocket is constructed which has 2 places) and $x = 0$ seats are sold; then the gain of the entrepreneur is -2. If $x = 1$ seat is sold, the gain is 0. If $x = 2$, 3, or 4 seats are sold, the gain is 2. By using Carnap's probabilities in order to compute the mathematical expectation (weighted arithmetic mean of gains and losses with the a priori probabilities as weights), we see that it will, under the given circumstances, be most profitable to construct a rocket which has $a = 2$ places. In this case the average gain, 1 money unit, is the highest.

The theory of action under uncertainty has received much stimulation through ideas borrowed from game theory (von Neumann and Morgenstern 1944), statistical decision theory (Wald 1950), and the theory of personal (subjective) probability (Savage 1954; Schlaiffer 1959).

III. Econometrics

Probability

Econometrics is an important special method for the evaluation of mathematical economic models in numerical terms and for the verification of economic theories; it uses the methods of modern statistics for this purpose. The importance of statistics for economics has been long recognized: "In connection with the process . . . of verification and the discovery of disturbing causes, or (to express the same idea differently) the discovery of the minor influences affecting economic phenomena, we find the proper place of statistics in economic reasoning" (Cairnes 1875, p. 85). "The deductive science of Economics must be verified and rendered useful by the purely empirical science of Statistics" (Jevons 1911, p. 22).

Modern statistics, which is based upon the theory of probability, may be described as applied probability. Probability (Nagel 1939) has been defined in various ways. The *classical* definition of probability defines it as the ratio between the number of favorable and the number of equally likely cases. Consider a die with six faces and the probability of throwing an ace. There is one favorable case and six equally likely cases. Hence the a priori probability is 1/6, according to the classical definition.

This definition is unsatisfactory, especially since it is in many cases very difficult, or even impossible, to determine what the equally likely cases are. A purely empirical definition of probability defines it as related to the *relative frequency* of events in a long series of trials. It may be conceived as the limit of this relative frequency as the number of trials increases indefinitely (R. von Mises 1951). Most statisticians follow Fisher, who defined probability as the relative frequency in an infinite hypothetical population. Kolmogoroff (1933) defines probability axiomatically in terms of modern set and measure theory

(Cramér 1946, pp. 137 ff.). To illustrate the axiomatic system of the probability calculus, take the following axioms of Fisz (1963, pp. 12–13).

Assume a set of elementary events: to every random event there corresponds a certain number, called its probability, which lies between zero and one; the probability of the sure event equals one; the probability of the alternative of the finite or denumerable infinite number of pairwise exclusive events is the sum of the probabilities of these events.

From these axioms follow a number of theorems: if a set of events exhausts the set of elementary events, their probability is one (certainty); the sum of the probabilities of any event and its complement is one; the probability of the impossible event is zero, and so on. This abstract concept of probability is then identified with relative frequency in certain random experiments.

Because of its great importance in recent discussions, we should be cognizant of *Bayes' theorem* (Lindley 1965, vol. 1, p. 20). Let B be some event and denote its probability by $p(B)$. Let $A_1, A_2, \ldots, A_n$ be a set of exclusive and exhaustive events and denote the probability of A_1 by $p(A_i)$. Furthermore, let $p(A_i/B)$ be the probability of A_i, given B, and $p(B/A_i)$ be the probability of B, given A_i. These are conditional probabilities. Then we have

$$p(A_i/B) = p(B/A_i)p(A_i)/p(B/A_1)p(A_1) + p(B/A_2)$$
$$p(A_2) + \ldots + p(B/A_n)p(A_n). \qquad (48)$$

To illustrate Bayesian methods, we take an example from Good (1965, pp. 12 ff.). Consider a simple sample where the result of N independent trials is either a success or a failure. Suppose we have obtained r successes and s failures $(r + s = N)$. Let p be the a priori probability of a success and $1 - p$ be the a priori probability of a failure. Assume that the sequence of trials is permutable (De Finetti 1937) — that is, a success does not depend upon the previous sequence of successes and failures. Good suggests for the estimation of p (a priori probability of success) a beta distribution, which is proportional to $p^a(1-p)^b$. The mathematical expectation of a success is, given r successes and s failures in a sample of N independent trials,

$$E = \frac{a+r+1}{a+b+N+2}. \tag{49}$$

This should be compared with Laplace's law of succession, which gives

$$L = \frac{r+1}{N+2}, \tag{50}$$

and with the maximum likelihood estimate of classical statistics,

$$M = r/N. \tag{51}$$

In contrast to the concept of statistical probability, related to relative frequency, one school of theoreticians considers a *logical concept* of probability, which is frequently called subjective or personal probability. The most important writers in this field are J. M. Keynes (1948), Ramsey (1928), Jeffreys (1948), De Finetti (1937), and, most recently, Savage (1954). See also Kryburg and Smockler (1964); Good (1965). Here probability is conceived as a logical concept, the rational degree of belief in a proposition based upon a certain amount of evidence. The "subjective" concept of probability, the degree of belief, has recently achieved some prominence (Savage 1962, Lindley 1965). The so-called Bayesian approach in statistics is essentially based upon it.

If probability is defined as being subjective then this concept is really a subject of psychology. If the subjective concept of probability is interpreted as ideal rational behavior, it seems that it is related to the logical concept of probability as developed by Carnap (1962).

The philosopher Carnap (1950; 1952) has pointed out that we should really distinguish between these two ideas of probability (the frequency concept and the logical concept) and that both are useful. In many scientific endeavors we utilize probability in the statistical sense as a quantity related to relative frequency, an empirical concept (Good 1965). On the other hand, it is also necessary to talk about the probability (in the logical sense) of a proposition or theory. Carnap (1962) and Kemeny (1963) have tried to lay the foundations for such a concept, which they call *degree of confirmation.* (See also Fels 1963; Tintner 1949.) A solution which would be practically useful in a science like physics or economics is still to be found. We can illustrate this concept by an example of Kemeny's (1963). We must have a certain "language" (in the semantic sense). Up to now the theory has only been developed for languages containing a finite number (or denumerable infinite number) of predicates. The full language of physics (or economics) cannot be included in the analysis. A model or interpretation of a logistic system must be defined. The number of models is infinite, and the domain of the individuals must be finite. If e is given as the sentence which stands for the evidence and h as the sentence which stands for the hypothesis, we can denote the degree of confirmation of the hypothesis h given the evidence e by $c(h,e)$.

The following conditions are imposed upon the degree of confirmation C:

CA1: C must define a system of betting which is coherent (fair) — (a) $0 \leq c(h,e) \leq 1$; (b) if h and e are logically equivalent to h' and e', then $c(h,e) = c(h',e')$; (c) if e logically implies h, then $c(h,e) = 1$; (d) if e logically implies the negation of (h and h'), then $c(h$ or $h',e) = c(h,e) + c(h',e)$; (e) $c(h$ and $e',e) = c(e',e) \cdot c(h,e$ and $e')$ where e and e' are not self contradictory.

In case we require strict coherence (fairness) (c) becomes $c(h,e) = 1$, if and only if e logically implies h. The concept of coherence (fairness) is defined as follows: Let $c(h,e) = r$, then the odds of a bet are $r/(1-r)$. In a coherent (fair) betting system (Ramsey 1928, De Finetti 1937) no profits are possible. Also the gambler can not be sure if he will win or lose. The case is then strict coherence (fairness)· (f) $c(h,e) = m(h$ and $e)/m(e)$.

Here m is a measure function. Equivalent sentences have the same measure. If h and h' are mutually exclusive, (d) becomes $m(h \text{ or } h') = m(h) + m(h')$. The set of models is disjoint, and the measure is additive. The measure of the set of all models is one, and the measure of the empty set is zero. Given a finite set and a measure which is additive: the measure of the universal set is one; of the empty set is zero, each measure is nonnegative; if the measure is defined over two subsets, it is also defined for all complements, sums, and products, and then it can be extended to all subsets. Hence only weights (measures) have to be assigned to models. If strict coherence is required, then $m(h) = 1$, only if h is analytic.

CA2: $c(h,e)$ is to depend only on the proposition expressed in h and e. We may select a minimal language, which allows for finiteness.

CA3: Constants which are logically alike can be treated a priori alike. This is the requirement of empiricism and is a version of the principle of indifference.

CA4: The definition of c must enable us to *learn from experience*. If we have a series of evidences consisting of more and more confirming instances, the c values must increase.

CA5: We need consider only that part of e which is relevant to h.

These conditions *CA1–5* are sufficient to solve a dice problem. The minimal language is the set of properties: $P_1, P_2, P_3, P_4, P_5, P_6$, (outcomes of the throw of the die). The number of throws (individuals) must be finite. The language L_n assigns one property P_i to each individual (throw). We then have 6^n models. How are the weights assigned? Let us say that the hypothesis is h_i; this means that the next throw will be P_i, and the evidence e^k states the outcome of the k previous throws. We have n individual constants a_i (throws). A sentence, $P_{i_1}a_1 . P_{i_2}a_2 \ldots P_{i_n}a_n$, is a state description.

By using Carnap's theory (1952), Kemeny comes to this important conclusion: That the degree of confirmation of the hypothesis h_i that the outcome of the next throw of the die will be P_i based upon the evidence e^k, that among k previous throws there have been k' throws with the result P_i and $k–k'$ throws with other results, depends only upon one single parameter L:

$$c(h_i, e^k) = \frac{k' + L/6}{k + L}. \tag{52}$$

L may be any non negative real number and may be interpreted as an index of caution. Consider the case where $k' = k$ — that is, where all previous throws are favorable. Then when $c = 1/2$, $k = (2/3)L$. This shows us after how many trials, all of them favorable, we can bet even money that the next throw will be P_i. If $L = 3$, we would do so after only 2 throws and after 200 consecutive successes if $L = 300$. The formula (52) may be written

$$c(h_i, e^k) = \frac{(k'/k) + (L/6k)}{1 + (L/k)}. \tag{53}$$

and we see that

$$\lim_{k \to \infty} c(h_i, e^k) = k'/k \tag{54}$$

For a long series of trials the "logical" factor L drops out, and the probability that the next throw will be a success is the relative frequency of successes, k'/k. This corresponds to the maximum likelihood estimate of classical statistics.

Carnap also points out that L may be considered a measure of our belief of how evenly we choose our alternatives. The less homogeneous the world is, the larger the optimal value of L. If $L = 0$, we have unbiased estimation in the statistical sense. A statistical estimate is unbiased, if its mean value (mathematical expectation, weighted arithmetic mean with the probabilities as weights) is equal to the parameter estimated in the unknown population. It would be best in a completely homogeneous world. If all k's of the k throws are aces, the probability of aces is one. Strict coherence (fairness) forbids this value.

Another interesting value is $L = \infty$, and $c = 1/6$ in Wittgenstein's method. Here we assign all state descriptions equal probability. Hence, the degree of confirmation is independent of past experience and forbidden by $CA4$, but it would be optimal in a world where individuals (throws) are evenly distributed among the 6 alternatives.

As a slight generalization, consider the problem of a K-faced die or a family of K (instead of 6) properties $P_1, P_2, \ldots, P_K$. Our formula becomes

$$c(h_i,e^k) = \frac{k' + L/K}{k+L}. \qquad (52')$$

Now, assume that $K = \infty$ — that is, a die with infinite number of faces.

$$c(h_i,e^k) = (k'/k)/\ 1 + (L/k) \qquad (53')$$

Again, what is the relation between L and K, if $k' = k$ — that is, if only favorable instances are observed? We have $L = k$ when $c = 1/2$ — that is, if $L = 1$, we will make an even bet that aces will turn up if only one ace has been observed. If $L = 10$, we will make an even bet on aces if we have 10 observations, all aces, and so on.

Laplace's rule of succession,

$$c(h_i,\ e^k) = (k'+1)/(k+2), \qquad (54')$$

must be restricted to simple alternatives — $K = 2$ to be consistent. This leads then to $L = 2$.

The problem of several families of predicates brings up some novel features of analogies (Carnap and Stegmueller 1958, p. 251 ff.) — for example, if balls of different colors and size are drawn from an urn, the combination of the two predicates, color and size, must be taken into account. This introduces another parameter. This problem is related to Nagel's (1939) problem of varieties of instances. Later work by Carnap (1963) connects his ideas with the subjective probability of Savage (1954).

It should be emphasized that the controversies about the foundations of probability are mostly of importance for the *interpretation* of probability statements. All writers in this field agree as far as the concrete laws of probability are concerned.

One branch of probability theory which has been very much developed in our time is the theory of *stochastic processes.* A stochastic process is a family of random variables depending upon a parameter (Fisz 1963, p. 272). There are many interesting applications in the fields of natural science but also in operations research. The applications in economics proper are still somewhat tentative. The use of the theory of stochastic processes in economics makes it possible to meet Hayek's objection (1952 pp. 61 ff.) that statistics cannot be applied to economics because our data must be samples of an unchanging population (see also F. M. Fisher 1960).

A stochastic process is stationary if its characteristics depend upon time differences and not upon absolute time. A stationary time series hence cannot have a trend; the variance and higher moments cannot change with time. For applications of stochastic processes to economics see Cootner (1964), Granger and Hatakana (1964).

An interesting application of a simple type of a stochastic process has been given by Blumen *et al.* (1955; see also Kemeny and Snell 1960, p. 199). It is based upon empirical data taken from social security records. The authors investigate empirically the transition probabilities of change between given occupational groups. Let $f(x, t: y, s)$ be the conditional probability (or probability density) when a random variable will have the value x at time t if it had the value y at time $s < t$: then this conditional probability is a transition probability. They find a remarkable agreement between the theoretically computed ultimate probability distribution and the empirical distribution. Similar methods have been used by Orcutt *et al.* (1961) for the analysis of various demographic problems — labor force, debt, and liquid asset behavior, and so on. (See also Kemeny and Snell [1962].)

We can take another example from operations research, which is, after all, nothing else but the econometrics of enterprise. This enterprise may be private or public. As a matter of fact, some

of the best work in this field has been done by French econometricians in close connection with experiences in nationalized
industries (Massé 1959; Lesourne 1960).

Consider a simple *queuing* process (Lindley 1965, vol. 1,
p. 187). Denote the probability that at time t there are n customers in the queue (including those who are being served) by
$p_n(t)$. In a small time interval Δt the probability that another
customer will join the queue is approximately $L(\Delta t)$, and the
probability that a customer will leave the queue is approximately $K(\Delta t)$. These probabilities are independent; L and K
are constants. As time passes, the queuing process can be shown
(under certain conditions) to settle down to a stationary situation which is quite independent of the initial situation. In the
limit (i.e., after a reasonably long lapse of time) we get limiting
probabilities. From these simple assumptions we may compute
the limiting probability distribution, which is given by

$$P_r = R^r P_0, \tag{55}$$

where $R = L/K < 1$ and $P_0 = 1 - R$. This is the limiting probability that the server is not occupied. The limiting distribution
is a geometric distribution, and R is the traffic intensity. With
average size of the queue expressed as $R/(1 - R)$, the expected
waiting time of a customer is in the limit $R/K(1 - R)$, and the
expected busy time is $(K - L)^{-1}$. More complicated queuing
processes have also been investigated. The methods are applicable to machine interference, and similar methods can be used
on problems of dams and storage (inventories).

Another example is the stochastic theory of *economic development* (Sengupta and Tintner 1963, 1964; Tintner and Thomas
1963). By following the theory of *economic stages* by Rostow
and others, we may approximate economic development by a
simple type of stochastic process in each stage of economic
development. This method has been applied to the data on
British industry compiled by Hoffman. The whole series covers
the period 1700 to 1939. The nature of the stochastic process at
each stage, assuming that it changes from stage to stage was
estimated. If only two types of regimes are recognized, the

change is estimated to have occurred in 1834; with three regimes we have an estimated change in 1791 and 1869. If we assume the existence of four types of economic development, the change occurred, according to our estimation, in 1777, 1820, and 1869.

In a recent paper (Tintner and Patel 1966) we have tried to apply the idea of a *lognormal diffusion process* to the theory of economic development. A random variable (in our case real national income) is lognormally distributed, if its *logarithm* follows the familiar bell-shaped normal distribution (Aitcheson and Brown 1957). By making some assumptions about the nature of the transition probabilities, we can derive a lognormal distribution where the logarithms of real national income are normally distributed, but the arithmetic mean and variance (a measure of dispersion) of the logarithm of national income are linear functions of time. Then, national income itself has an exponential trend. This theory is verified and parameters of the process are estimated with the help of the method of maximum likelihood on the basis of Indian data, 1948–61. As a tentative application to policy, we also assume that government expenditure influences the transition probabilities in a simple way. Then the trend of national income becomes a function of total government expenditure. On the basis of this model we make predictions about the trend of Indian national income, assuming various plausible developments for future government expenditure.

Dynamic programming (Bellman 1957) is also most promising for the treatment of dynamic economic problems (Boulding 1950; Holt, Modigliani, Muth, and Simon 1960).

Models of this type make it possible to rationally treat problems of planning production, employment, and inventories for large private corporations. Also, there is the possibility of utilizing similar models in economic planning for a whole economy.

Statistics

Probability theory (and with it statistics, which is applied probability) finds itself in some predicaments today. There is still a large number of statisticians who cling to the traditional conception of probability, defined as being related to empirical relative frequency in the long run or in large (theoretically infinite) samples. There is, however, a growing movement toward the Bayesian point of view (Schlaiffer 1959). Traditional statisticians are reluctant to use this theorem, since from a classical point of view the conditions for its application are hardly ever present. The Bayesian point of view is connected with a revival of the notion of personal probability (Kryburg and Smockler, 1954) denoting the subjective belief of the investigator. If this belief is truly personal or subjective, it would make probability theory and statistics a subject for psychological investigation. This is also suggested by the large use of introspection and experimentation in this field. If, on the other hand, personal probability signifies the rational point of view then perhaps it must be interpreted in a sense like the Carnap's (1962) theory of the degree of confirmation.

The movement is still largely influenced by the purely pragmatic point of view of decision theory (Wald 1950, games against nature). The justification of the decision outlook in industrial and perhaps, some other applications cannot be denied. On the other hand, the particular method of reaching decisions (e.g., by the minimax principle), may appear more doubtful. But how can decision theory be applied in the field of scientific investigation, where the losses connected with various types of errors can hardly be taken for granted (R. A. Fisher 1956, pp. 99 ff.)? Also, in the field of econometrics the application of decision theory appears doubtful in view of the possible failure of welfare economics to produce on acceptable welfare function. Here, as in many other fields of application, the appropriateness of the decision theoretic point of view is questionable.

Because of its great importance for econometrics, we must make a more detailed examination of modern statistics. Since modern statistics is firmly based upon probability theory, a strict distinction must be made between the concrete empirical sample and the universe or population from which it is taken.

The fundamental ideas of modern statistics are applicable in econometrics, but they cannot be applied blindly or by analogy.

In many applications (agricultural experimentation, industrial experimentation, biological, and especially genetic applications) carefully planned experiments are possible. This is not true for economics, however, except in a very few cases. Hence, while in ordinary econometric work the fundamental ideas of modern statistics must be used, the specific methods useful with designed experiments (e.g., analysis of variance) are not necessarily applicable.

We use sampling methods to get information about a given universe or population. A random sample must be taken in such a way that each item in the population has the same chance of being chosen. More refined methods of sampling, like stratified sampling or systematic sampling are also useful for the collection of economic data.

To sample a numerical characteristic of a given population, say the expenditure on food by the urban population of Austria, care must be taken that every family has the same chance of being chosen as a member of the sample. This may be achieved by numbering all families and then by choosing the families in the sample with the help of a table of random numbers.

The fundamental problem of statistics is: given a sample, how can we derive inferences about an unknown population? A complete census would give us information about the numerical characteristic of which we are interested (the expenditure on food by the urban population of Austria); but since such a census is costly and frequently not feasible, we must use methods of sampling. The most fundamental method is estimation.

To estimate a characteristic of the unknown population (the average expenditure on food by the urban Austrian population), we compute a function of the observed values of our *sample* — for example, the arithmetic mean or median in the sample. To sample expenditure on food, let $x_1, x_2, \ldots, x_n$ be the food expenditure of the n families in a random sample. Then the sample mean $M = (x_1 + x_2 + \ldots + x_n)/n$ is the average food expenditure of the families in the sample. The median is computed as follows: The items are ordered according to size. In odd numbered samples items in the middle constitute the median, and in an even numbered sample the median is the arithmetic mean of the two items in the middle. What properties of statistical estimates are desirable so that we may choose between various possibilities?

We want the empirical estimate to be consistent. An estimator is consistent if it converges in probability to the parameter of the population estimated (Wilks 1962, p. 351). By convergence in probability we mean the following (Wilks 1962, p. 99): Consider a set of random variables (e.g., our estimators). The event that the value of our estimator deviates from the parameter in the population by more than a given (small) number is investigated. If the probability of this event tends to zero, as the sample becomes larger and larger, we have convergence in probability. If we sample from a normal population, which has a bell-shaped symmetrical probability density, for example, the arithmetic mean of a random sample is a consistent estimate of the mathematical expectation — that is, of the mean value of the unknown normal population. If we assume that the food expenditure by the Austrian urban population has a normal distribution, then the arithmetic mean of food expenditure of a random sample of families is a consistent estimate of the population mean — that is, the true (unknown) mean of food expenditure by the population of urban Austrian families.

Another property is *unbiasedness* of estimation (Cramér 1946, pp. 351 ff.). The mean value (mathematical expectation) of the estimate is equal to the estimated parameter in the population. Practically, this means that if many estimates of a given sample size are available and we compute the arithmetic mean of the estimates, the chances are that this general mean will deviate from the true value of the estimated parameter in the unknown population by a small number. The property of unbiasedness has been criticized by Carnap (1952) and also from a Bayesian point of view by Lindley (1965, vol. 1, pp. 130 ff.).

Under certain circumstances, the unbiased estimate (e.g., the arithmetic mean of the sample) will itself have a tendency to be normally distributed, at least in large samples. Such a distribution can be characterized by its mean value and by its variance, which measures the dispersion about the mean. A consistent estimate is *efficient* if (for a given sample size) its variance is as small as possible. Assume that we have a (large) random sample of n items from a normal population. The variance of this population is σ^2. The variance of the arithmetic mean of our random sample is σ^2/n. The sample mean is a consistent estimate of the population mean and is also unbiased: its own mathematical expectation is equal to the estimated parameter in the population.

To compute the sample median, the sample is ordered according to size and (for an odd n) the item in the middle or (for an even n) the arithmetic mean of the two items in the center is chosen. Again, this is a consistent estimate. It tends to be normally distributed for large samples. The variance of the sample median (for large samples) is $1.57\,\sigma^2/n$. Hence the sample mean is a more efficient estimate. Assume we have a sample of $n = 100$ items; then we must have a sample of $n = 157$ to achieve the same accuracy for the sample median as for the arithmetic mean, if we measure accuracy by the variance.

Sufficiency (Wilks 1962, p. 351) is a more complicated characteristic of statistical estimates. A sufficient estimate has the property that the conditional distribution of any other estimator, given the sufficient estimate, is independent of the estimated parameter. The arithmetic mean of a sample taken from a normal population with unknown mathematical expectation but known variance is sufficient. The distribution of any other estimator (e.g., the sample median), given a knowledge of the sufficient estimate (sample mean), is independent of the estimated parameter (mathematical expectation in the population). Sufficient statistics are of particular importance in the Bayesian approach (Savage 1962, Lindley 1965, vol. 2, p. 46 ff.)

The most important procedure of estimation in econometrics is R. A. Fisher's method of *maximum likelihood*. It is based upon the idea of choosing from the infinite number of possible values of the unknown parameter in the population the one which has, in view of the given sample, the highest chance to have produced the empirical sample. Unbiased estimates correspond to the arithmetic mean and maximum likelihood estimates to the mode. The mode is the value which has the highest probability or probability density. Under some conditions the results of maximum likelihood estimation are consistent and efficient for large samples; on the other hand, although they are not generally unbiased, they have the desirable property of being invariant against (non-singular) transformations, which is not in general true of unbiased estimates. For instance the maximum likelihood estimate of the standard deviation in the population, which is the square root of the population variance, will be the square root of the maximum likelihood estimate of the variance. The unbiased estimate of the standard deviation, however, is not, in general, the square root of the unbiased estimate of the variance.

In the modern Bayesian approach the method of maximum likelihood is justified as a convenient approximation (Savage 1954, pp. 224 ff.; Lindley 1965, vol. 2, pp. 128 ff.). For example, from a stratified sample of urban families in Austria (1954–5), consisting of 7,019 families, I have estimated the income elasticity of food expenditure by the method of maximum likelihood (Tintner 1960c, p. 36). The estimated income elasticity is 0.46. By making certain assumptions about the distribution of the elasticity in the unknown population, I chose, as my estimate, the population which had the maximum likelihood to produce the given sample. This figure should be interpreted as follows: If *ceteris paribus* (especially with unchanging prices and tastes) the income of the urban population in Austria increases by 1 per cent, we may expect an increase in expenditure on food by about 0.46 per cent — that is, among all possible unknown populations characterized by different income elasticities the one with the given income elasticity is the most likely to have produced the empirical sample.

Another important method of estimation which yields unbiased estimates is that of *least squares*. Here an estimate is found by making a minimum of the sum of squares of the deviation of the observations in the sample from the estimated value. The results of maximum likelihood estimation and the estimation by the method of least squares are frequently (but not always) identical. In our example, for instance, the estimate of the income elasticity as 0.46 per cent is also the estimate obtained by the method of least squares.

In econometrics, as in other applications of statistics, we frequently desire not only single estimates (point estimates) but also regions into which the estimated parameter may fall with given probability (e.g., 95 per cent). There are two methods, which in most cases will lead to the same numerical results, but have different interpretations (Fraser 1961). In our example, *fiducial limits* for the elasticity with 95 per cent probability are 0.49 and 0.44. The fiducial probability of 95 per cent leads to the conclusion that the unknown universe of the urban population in Austria from which our sample is taken will react as follows, *ceteris paribus*, to an increase of income by 1 per cent: Food expenditure will increase by not less than 0.44 per cent and not more than 0.49 per cent (Tintner 1960*c*, p. 38). A similar interpretation might be given from the Bayesian point of view (Lindley 1965, vol. 2, p. 15).

Fiducial probability is a concept related to logical probability and cannot be interpreted in the frequency sense; hence many statisticians object to it. In contrast to Fisher, Neymann (1938) considers one single population with a single unknown parameter to be estimated; for example, our income elasticity in the unknown universe of the urban population of Austria. He contemplates, however, a statistician who makes estimates very frequently and computes limits for his estimates — here called *confidence limits*. These limits are random variables since they are functions of the items in the sample which are themselves random variables. The limits will sometimes include the estimated (constant) parameter of the population (the true income elasticity) — sometimes not. It is these limits, which are random or chance variables. Suppose the statistician fixes the limits in such a fashion that they will include the unknown parameter in 95 per cent of all cases and the parameter will fall outside the limits in only 5 per cent of all cases. Then, we will obtain exactly the same limits as before, but their meaning is different.

From a strictly Bayesian point of view we might derive different limits (Schlaiffer 1959, pp. 661 ff.).

Our limits, now interpreted as confidence limits, show that there is only one unknown population, characterized by the unknown true parameter in the universe (income elasticity). If we determine limits by methods that have a probability of 95 per cent (now interpreted in the frequency sense) of including the parameter in a long series of trials, the limits are 0.44 and 0.49.

Another important idea is R. A. Fisher's concept of *test of significance*. Here we test a hypothesis called the null hypothesis (e.g., the hypothesis that the income elasticity in the unknown population is zero). What are the chances that in the unknown universe as income increases there will be *no* reaction as far as food expenditure is concerned? To test this hypothesis we must arbitrarily fix a level of significance — that is, a probability which is such that the null hypothesis will be rejected if the sample could have been obtained with a smaller probability. Assume a level of significance of 1 per cent — that is, we will reject all null hypothesis with a probability of less than 1 per cent. On the other hand, we will not reject null hypotheses which could have arisen with a probability of more than 1 per cent. It is unlikely, on the basis of our sample, that the urban population in Austria will not change its food expenditure if income increases. Thus, the test of our null hypothesis gives us a probability which is much smaller than 1 per cent or even than 0.1 per cent; hence, we may reject the null hypothesis (Tintner 1960c, p. 40). Significance tests have been treated by Lindley (1965, vol. 2, p. 58 ff.) from a Bayesian point of view.

There is a divergence among statisticians about testing hypotheses. Neymann (1938) and E. S. Pearson not only consider the probability of rejecting a true hypothesis (level of significance — called errors of the first kind, Lehmann 1959) but also consider the existence of rival hypotheses. The error committed in not rejecting a false hypothesis is called an error of the second kind. The method recommended by Neymann and Pearson and adopted by most statisticians is to keep the probability of committing an error of the first kind (rejecting a true hypothesis) on a given level (level of significance, e.g. 1 per cent) and then to construct the test in such a way as to minimize the chance of not rejecting a false hypothesis (committing an error of the second kind: Kendall and Stuart 1961, pp. 161 ff.).

Here all probabilities are interpreted in the frequency sense. Let us test in our example the hypothesis that in the unknown population the income elasticity for food expenditure by the urban population in Austria is 1. Our hypothesis then states that in the population, as income increases by a given percentage, the urban Austrians will react by increasing food expenditure by the same percentage. By constructing a test in the manner of Neymann and Pearson, we find that this hypothesis must be rejected at the level of significance of 1 per cent (Tintner 1960*c*, pp. 41–42.). It is unlikely that the urban population in Austria will react in the indicated manner to a percentage increase in income, *ceteris paribus*, by increasing food expenditure by the same percentage.

Neymann and Pearson's method may also be defended from the point of view of decision theory. Wald (1950) has generalized this method to a general method of decision functions (Lehmann 1959; Braithwaite 1953, pp. 196 ff.). Assume that there are various actions possible (rejection of a hypothesis, non-rejection, or continuing the experiment) and that we know the losses which all the actions incur. Then we may compute the probabilities connected with each action and find the mathematical expectation of the loss. This risk function should then be minimized. This idea is especially important in connection with industrial experimentation and some methods of operations research. The Bayesian approach (De Finetti 1937; Savage 1954; 1962; Lindley 1965; Kryburg and Smockler 1964) bases itself firmly upon the personalist or subjective concept of probability. In a sense these ideas are related to decision theory, and many of the classical ideas of statistics, described above, appear questionable from this point of view.

Methodology of Econometrics

Econometrics, the result of a certain outlook on the role of economics, consists of the application of mathematical statistics to economic data to lend empirical support to the models constructed by mathematical economics and to obtain numerical results (Tintner 1952, p. 3; 1960c, p. 1).

The models which are utilized in econometrics depend upon the special scope of the investigation. This, in turn, will be mostly influenced by the policy purposes which the econometrician has in mind. Although there may be partial equilibrium models in econometrics (e.g., the investigation of a given market in isolation), models of general equilibrium, which try to analyze the interaction of many economic variables in a given national economy, are more important. Also, the models can be classified into static models, where time plays no particular part, and dynamic models, where time enters in a significant fashion into the analysis. Such models will in general involve lagged values of the economic variables. For instance, a dynamic model of a given economy will involve not only contemporary prices but also prices of previous years.

Mathematical economics in its modern form develops models for individual households and firms. From this point of view it is already useful for applications in market research and operations research (the econometrics of the enterprise). It is also possible to combine these results and study, under certain (not always very realistic) assumptions, questions which pertain to a total economy. If we want to study these problems econometrically (i.e., with the help of statistical methods), we need aggregates or index numbers for practical reasons. The number of households and firms is too great to permit the study of even the simplest relations between all of them, even with the help of the biggest existing (or easily imaginable) electronic computers. The problem of the appropriate construction of aggregates or index numbers is one of the most difficult but evidently fundamental one in econometrics. Stone (1947) and Tintner (1952, pp. 102 ff.) have proposed purely statistical criteria,

which are based upon Hotelling's idea of principal components—a method closely related to factor analysis.

The practical interest in aggregation in econometric work
based upon the theories of Keynes (1936) which are essentially
macro-economic (i.e., deal with aggregates) stimulated much
important theoretical work, especially by American and French
mathematical economists (see Green 1964). The problem was
further considered by Theil (1954), who, however, dealt only
with linear aggregation and introduced statistical as well as
theoretical considerations. He has shown the difficulty of perfect
aggregation, and he and his school have followed certain ideas
of Frisch and Wald (see Pfanzagl 1955) and used statistical
methods for the construction of aggregates or index numbers
which have certain optimal properties (Theil 1954; 1962).

Prais and Houttakker (1955, p. 13 ff.) have considered lognormal distributions in the theory of aggregation. A variable is
said to be lognormally distributed if its logarithm follows the
well known bell-shaped normal or Gaussian distribution. For
instance, let y be consumption and x income. The individual
consumption functions are

$$y_i = a + b \log x_i \tag{59}$$

for individual or family $i(i = 1, 2, \ldots, n)$. Also, a and b are
constants. Total consumption may be written in the form

$$y = na + bn \log x^*, \tag{60}$$

if we assume that income (x) is lognormally distributed and
x^* is the *geometric* mean of the individual incomes x_1. Let x_1,
$x_2, \ldots, x_n$ be the income of n families. The geometric mean
(defined only for positive incomes) is

$$x^* = \sqrt[n]{x_1, x_2, \ldots, x_n}. \tag{61}$$

For an application of information theory to aggregation see
Theil (1967).

One fundamental problem in econometrics is the division

of variables into two classes. Endogenous variables are economic variables whose interaction determines the economic system; for example, quantities sold and bought, interest rates, and so on. The number of endogenous variables must normally be equal to the number of equations in the system in question. In addition, there are the predetermined variables — variables which influence the system but are not influenced by it (exogenous variables like the weather and lagged values of the endogenous variables like past prices).

After constructing a model, the econometrician has to make certain assumptions about the stochastic nature of the equations involved. Broadly speaking, he has to evaluate errors in the variables (akin to errors of observations, Morgenstern 1963) and errors in the equations (i.e., the effect of economic variables which are left out of given equations and are replaced by stochastic variables). Other assumptions of a statistical or probability nature have also to be made; for example, independence of the stochastic variables over time.

Before statistical estimation of the postulated relationships can be discussed, the problem of *identification* must be considered. Simon (1957, p. 10 ff.) sees this from the general point of view of an analysis of causal relations as the following: Given the model and the stochastic assumptions involved, is it possible (in principle) to estimate the individual relationships (or even individual parameters) in the hypothetical case where we have infinite samples?

To illustrate the particular idea of causal relationships used in econometrics, we present the following example taken from Simon (1957; see also Wold 1965). Denote an index measuring the favorableness of the weather for growing wheat by x_1, the size of the wheat crop by x_2, and the price of wheat by x_3. The system, assumed to be linear for the sake of simplicity, can thus be stated as

$$a_{11}x_1 = a_{10}, \tag{62}$$

$$a_{21}x_1 + a_{22}x_2 = a_{20}, \tag{63}$$

and

$$a_{32}x_2 + a_{33}x_3 = a_{30}. \tag{64}$$

Here a_{ij} are constants. No stochastic terms are introduced. This model might be stated in the form: x_1 (state of the weather) is the direct cause of x_2 (wheat crop); and x_2 (wheat crop) is the direct cause of x_3 (price of wheat). It should be noted that this causal relation is established by observing which variables appear in a given equation. This idea of causal relations has been much discussed in recent years (Liu 1960; Strotz and Wold 1960).

As an example, consider a Marshallian market of partial equilibrium. Denote the price of commodity in question by P and the quantity exchanged by Q. Let a_{ij} be some constants to be estimated and assume as a first approximation that the relations involved are linear. The demand function is

$$a_{10} + a_{11}P + a_{12}Q = u_1, \qquad (65)$$

and the supply function is

$$a_{20} + a_{21}P + a_{22}Q = u_2. \qquad (66)$$

The stochastic variables u_1 and u_2 are errors in the equations. In the demand function (65) we consider a linear relationship between the price and the quantity of the given commodity, but there are other variables which enter into the demand relation; for example, income, prices of complementary and competing commodities, and so on. If the individual influences of all these neglected variables are small and irregular, we may replace them all by the stochastic variable u_1. Similarly the supply equation (66) is conceived in first approximation as a linear relationship between the price and the quantity of the commodity in question, but there are other factors which influence the supply of the commodity and are here omitted (technological conditions, cost conditions, prices of the factors of production, etc.). All these omitted variables are replaced by the stochastic variable u_2.

Now, consider the identification of the demand function (65) without making assumptions about the random variables u_1

and u_2. Our system consists of two endogenous variables P and Q, and thus also of two linear equations which in equilibrium determine these two variables. There are no predetermined variables.

Multiply the first equation (65), the demand equation, by an arbitrary constant K_1 and the second equation (66), the supply equation, by an arbitrary constant K_2. This linear combination of the demand and the supply equation (which is economically meaningless) is

$$K_1a_{10} + K_2a_{20} + (K_1a_{11} + K_2a_{21})P + (K_1a_{12} + K_2a_{22})Q = K_1u_1 + K_2u_2. \tag{67}$$

Can we distinguish this meaningless linear combination of the demand and the supply function (67) from the true demand function (65)? Evidently, this is not possible within our model. One must remember that all we know from (65) about the demand function is that it is a linear relation between price (P) and quantity (Q) with a random variable u_1. Since the linear combination (67) is of the same form, we have a linear combination of price and quantity with random variables $K_1u_1 + K_2u_2$. Hence we say that in our model the demand function (65) is not identified. Koopmans (see Hood and Koopmans 1953, pp. 27 ff.) has given rules for identification, and a statistical test for identification has also been supplied by Basmann (1960).

Having satisfied ourselves that a given relationship in the model is identified, there arises the problem of statistical estimation. A number of methods have been proposed in this field. The *full maximum likelihood method* is in almost all cases so complicated that one has to use numerical approximation. If we use the full maximum likelihood method, we maximize the probability of obtaining the given sample, taking all restrictions implied by the model into account. As a substitute, the *limited information method* of Anderson and Rubin (1949) or the *two stage least squares method* of Theil (1961, pp. 334 ff.) and Basmann (1957) sometimes can be used.

In estimating a single equation by the method of limited information, we neglect all the properties of the total system except the following: Which endogenous and predetermined variables enter into the equation which is to be estimated and which predetermined variables are in the system but not in the equation?

If we use the two stage least square method we first compute the reduced form equations — that is, we estimate by the method of least squares the linear relations between each one of the endogenous variables in the equation to be estimated and all the predetermined variables, both those in the equation and also the predetermined variables in the system but not in the equation. Then we utilize the estimated values of the endogenous variables in the equation to estimate the original equation, again by the method of least squares.

As an example, let us consider a model proposed by Tintner (1952, pp. 166 ff.) and treated by various methods of estimation by Goldberger (1964, pp. 328 ff., 344 ff.). Denote the quantity of meat consumed per capita by Q, a price index of meat by P, disposable income per capita by Y, unit cost of meat processing by C, and an index of cost of agricultural production by K. The data are taken from United States agricultural statistics, 1919–41. For simplicity all variables are deviations from their means so that constant terms can be omitted in the equations. The model is

$$Q = a_1 P + a_2 Y + u_1. \tag{68}$$

This is the demand equation for meat. It assumes that in the first approximation the demand for meat depends linearly upon the price of meat and disposable income. The variable u_1 is a random variable and stands for other economic factors which influence the demand for meat (e.g., prices of other commodities). These are omitted and replaced by the stochastic variable u_1. Also a_1 and a_2 are constants to be estimated. The supply equation is

$$Q = b_1 P + b_2 C + b_3 K + u_2. \tag{69}$$

Again, the supply of meat is assumed in first approximation to depend in a linear fashion upon the price of meat, the cost of meat processing, and the cost of agricultural production. The random variable u_2 stands for all other factors which influence the supply of meat (*e.g.*, the weather). Here our aim is to estimate the constants b_1, b_2, b_3. Note that we have a system of two linear relations and two endogenous variables — Q the quantity of meat consumed and P the price of meat. These are simultaneously determined in equilibrium through the interaction of our two equations. We also have, however, 3 variables which are assumed to be predetermined. They influence the market of meat but are not influenced by it, under our assumptions. They are Y disposable income, C cost of processing meat, K cost of agricultural production. It should be emphasized that in this model, as in many other econometric models, the predetermined variables are not really exogenous because part of the disposable income Y will be generated in the meat market. The variables are assumed only to be predetermined for the purpose of studying this particular market.

The reduced form equations give the linear relations between each endogenous variable (Q and P) and all the predetermined variables (Y, C, and K). They have been estimated by the method of least squares:

$$q = -0.030839Y - 0.344626C + 0.613660K \qquad (70)$$

and

$$p = 0.096075Y + 0.208343C - 0.033902K.$$

Since we have just enough conditions for the identification of the supply equation (69), we may estimate it by the *indirect method of least squares.* We simply eliminate from the system (70) the variable Y, which does not appear in the supply equation (69). We obtain an estimate of the supply equation:

$$Q = -0.32P - 0.28C + 0.60K. \qquad (71)$$

For the demand equation (68) we have more conditions than are necessary for identification, hence, it is *overidentified.*

The simplest method of elimination (indirect least squares) is not applicable. By applying the method of two stage least squares (Theil 1961, pp. 334 ff.; Basmann (1957), we use the estimated value of p from (70) in equation (69) and compute the following estimate for the supply function for meat:

$$q = -1.58p + 0.20Y. \tag{72}$$

Again, this has been obtained by the method of least squares. On the other hand, the limited information method of Anderson and Rubin (1949) gives a different estimate:

$$Q = 4.85P + 0.53Y. \tag{73}$$

Johnston (1963, p. 269) has computed a *consumption function* for the United Kingdoms, 1948–58. With C_t as consumption and Y_t as disposable income and by using the method of limited information, he obtained

$$C_t = 3,841 + 0.4923Y_t; \tag{74}$$

and with the application of two stage least squares the result was

$$C_t = 2,041 + 0.6029Y_t. \tag{75}$$

The marginal propensity to consume is estimated in the first case as about $1/2$ and in the second case as about $3/5$. The results of various econometric estimation methods are frequently quite different since they are based upon different theoretical assumptions. Since the small sample properties of these estimates are not yet sufficiently explored, it is difficult to say which method is preferable (Basmann 1960; Johnston 1963, pp. 275 ff.).

A convenient method of analysis are the *recursive* systems of Wold (1953, pp. 28 ff.), which arise if the matrix of contemporaneous endogenous variables becomes triangular. These ideas can be illustrated by a simple example from Tintner's (1960, pp. 252 ff.) Austrian data, 1948–55. Denote the logarithm of the quantity by X_{1t} and the logarithm of the price of pork in the year t by X_{2t}. We assume that the supply of pork depends upon the price of the year before, but that the demand is a relation between the price and the quantity of pork in the same year. Then, if the errors or deviations of the two equations are independent, we may estimate them in this form by the classical method of least squares: thus,

$$X_{1t} = 0.81 + 0.74X_{2t-1} \qquad (76)$$

and

$$X_{2t} = 0.80 - 0.15X_{1t}. \qquad (77)$$

The first of these equations (76) is the supply function, and the second (77) is the demand function. If the price of pork is known in a given year, we may compute the supply for the next year from (76); and by using the result in equation (77), we compute the price for the subsequent year, and so on. The system (76) and (77) forms a *causal chain*.

F. M. Fisher (1961) has established proximity theorems and shows that the customary assumptions for identification of simultaneous equations system also hold as approximations if the a priori restrictions are close approximations, omitted variables have small coefficients, endogenous variables have negligible effect on the assumed exogenous variables, and endogenous variables have negligible indirect effect on the assumed exogenous variables. An interesting method for estimation of simultaneous econometric equations has been proposed by F. M. Fisher (1966). He starts with the idea of block recursive systems, which is in fact a generalization of Wold's recursive systems (1965), illustrated above. Then he makes some reasonable assumptions about the errors in the equations. The estimation is effected by the use of instrumental variables (Malinvaud 1963, pp. 352 ff.; Christ 1966, pp. 402 ff.). Instrumental variables are uncorrelated with the disturbances and are chosen by taking the casual relations with the variables in the equation to be estimated into account. Fisher gives a method of classifying these instrumental variables and choosing them in the most advantageous way. In our discussion of the estimation of econometric models we have neglected all problems not connected with errors in the equations. Even there, difficult problems of estimation occur if the model includes lagged values of the endogenous variables and also if the errors in the equations are not independent over time but show autocorrelations. Since economic data are rarely as accurate as one is prone to assume (Morgenstern 1963), we will invariably meet with errors in the variables, akin to errors of observations. These errors constitute a difficult problem in the estimation of econometric relations. They may also give rise to the problem of multicollinearity (Frisch 1934; Tintner 1952, pp. 121 ff.) — the situation where (approximate) linear relations exist between the "independent" variables in a least squares problem.

Various methods are available to deal with the problems arising when autocorrelations or serial correlations between the errors or deviations exist (Tintner 1952, part 3). Autocorrelation measures the relationship between lagged values of the same random variable, and serial correlation measures the relationship between the values of one random variable and the lagged value of another random variable. Not much is known about the treatment of these problems in small samples, but for stationary time series (i.e., time series without trend) some modern methods of spectral analysis (Hannan 1960; Granger and Hatakana 1964) may be applicable.

Prediction

Prediction in economics is not easy. An amusing list of wrong predictions by some great economists of the past is contained in Zweig (1950, p. 25 ff.). It includes Adam Smith, Malthus, Senior, Say, Ricardo, Sismondi, Mill, Marx, Keynes. It seems that the besetting sin of economists is the inclination to project existing situations and tendencies of their own time and society into the future. It is ultimately the goal of econometrics to achieve reliable predictions. Such predictions are of great scientific interest, as tentative verifications of economic models and theories.

But they are also of importance for applications to economic policy.

It cannot be denied that up to now prediction with the help of econometric methods has not been too successful. This point of view has been stated forcefully by Machlup (1955, p. 19):

> Where the economist's prediction is *conditional*, that is, based upon specific conditions, but where it is not possible to check the fulfilment of all the conditions stipulated, the underlying theory cannot be disconfirmed, whatever the outcome observed. Nor is it possible to disconfirm a theory where the prediction is made with a *stated probability* value less than 100%; for, if an event is predicted with, say, 70% probability, any kind of outcome is consistent with the prediction. Only if the same "case" were to occur hundreds of times could we verify the stated probability by the frequency of "hits" and "misses." This does not mean complete frustration of all attempts to verify our economic theories. But it does mean that the tests of most our theories will be more nearly of the character of *illustrations* than of verifications of the kind possible in relation with repeatable controlled experiments or with recurring fully-identified situations.

An excellent survey of forecasting is contained in Theil (1961 pp. 49 ff.). He utilizes American, Dutch, Norwegian, Swedish, Danish, Canadian, and West German forecasts, both private and public. He comes to the conclusion that forecasts almost invariably underestimate change. This is particularly important for questions of policy. There it is necessary to predict the exogenous variables — that is, the variables which influence the economic system but are not influenced by it. If biased forecasts are used for policy purposes, they will naturally lead to losses in welfare.

It has sometimes been maintained that predictions in economics are impossible in principle since these very predictions, if they are believed by the acting economic subjects, will falsify the original predictions. Grunberg and Modigliani (1954; see also Simon 1957, pp. 79 ff.) have investigated the old problem of prediction in economics and the question of whether public prediction can influence the eventual outcome of the economic process. They come to the following conclusion:

It has been shown that, provided that correct private prediction is possible, correct public prediction is also conceptually possible. Two possibilities may be distinguished (1) The public prediction does not affect the course of events because the agents are indifferent to or incapable of reacting to the public prediction. In this case, correct public prediction coincides with correct private prediction. (2) Agents react to public prediction, and their reaction alters the course of events. The reaction can conceptually be known and taken into account. It has been shown that boundedness of the variables of the predictive system and the continuity over the relevant interval of the functions relating the variables to each other are sufficient, though not necessary conditions for the existence of correct public predictions. These conditions were found to be normally fulfilled in the world about which predictive statements are to be made. The argument of this paper establishes the falsity of the proposition that the agents' reaction to public prediction necessarily falsifies all such predictions and that, therefore, social scientists may never hope to predict both publicly and correctly. But it demonstrates no more than that correct public prediction is possible if the possibility of correct private prediction is accepted. About the possibility of private prediction it has nothing to say. So, in the end, the major difficulties of prediction in the domain of social prediction turn out to be those of private prediction.

We (Hohenbalken and Tintner 1962) have constructed a small static model for the United States, using national income data for the period 1948–60. The endogenous variables are those which are simultaneously determined by the interaction of the equations of the system. Here there are only 5 endogenous variables: C is personal nominal consumption expressed in current dollars, which, represents the total value of all goods and services consumed. Y is the nominal gross national product, which represents the total value of all commodities produced. P is the price index of the gross national product, which shows the general movement of the price level. D is total employment, the sum of total civilian, agricultural and non-agricultural employment — that is, the number of people employed in all civilian occupations. X is real national income, national income expressed in constant dollar values derived by dividing nominal national income (Y) by an appropriate price index (P).

The system, of course, is also influenced by other (exogenous) variables: N is the population of the United States. G is nominal public consumption, the total consumption of federal and state as well as local authorities. *I*, which is nominal gross asset formation, expresses private investment. *L*, nominal increases in stocks, is the total change in the value of inventories. *E* is nominal exports and *M* nominal imports, expressing the dollar value of international trade. *W* is nominal yearly wage per worker (hourly earnings in manufacturing times weekly average of hours worked in manufacturing times 52); Time is t. It should be emphasized that some of these variables are not really exogenous to the functioning of the American economic system, but they have been assumed to be exogenous and would become endogenous in a larger dynamic system like the one of Klein and Goldberger (1957; see also Duesenberry *et al.* 1965). Our purpose was to construct a small model which would be immediately comparable to other similar models of Western European countries and Canada (von Hohenbalken and Tintner 1962).

By using the method of simultaneous equations, we derived the following estimates of the equations in our system:

$$C_t/N_tP_t = 687.9 + 0.336\, Y_t/N_tP_t. \tag{78}$$

This is a Keynesian type consumption function. It relates real consumption per head $(C_t/N_t\, P_t)$ to real national income per head (Y_t/N_tP_t) linearly. Our estimate of the marginal propensity to consume is 0.336. This means that if real national income per capita increases by \$1.00, real per capita consumption may be expected to increase by about \$0.34. The next equation is simply a bookkeeping definition of nominal national income:

$$Y_t = C_t + G_t + I_t + L_t + E_t - M_t. \tag{79}$$

We have the obvious definition of real national income:

$$X_t = Y_t/P_t. \tag{80}$$

Real national income is nominal national income divided by a suitable index of the price level.

The demand for labor is determined by the marginal productivity of labor:

$$dX_t/dD_t = W_t/P_t. \qquad (81)$$

This follows from the theory of production under free competition and neglects the monopolistic elements in the American economy. Under free competition it can be shown that if a firm maximizes its profits with given prices and wages, the maximum of profits implies the condition that the marginal productivity of each factor of production is equal to the ratio between the price of this factor and the price of the product. To understand our concept of marginal productivity consider, *ceteris paribus*, a small increase in the amount of one factor used; the the corresponding increase of the product will be the marginal productivity. The last equation is a primitive production function of the Cobb-Douglas type. Such functions are linear in the logarithm of the product and the factors of production. It has been estimated by the method of simultaneous equations by using the assumption of free competition. Here again we neglect the monopolistic elements and, for example, the existence of trade unions thus,

$$\log X_t = 6.652 + 0.630 \log D_t. \qquad (82)$$

It should also be noted that in this static model capital has been neglected. The estimated coefficient 0.63 is an elasticity, thus if employment in the United States increases by 1 per cent we may expect an increase of production of about 0.63 per cent.

To utilize this non-linear model for problems of economic policy (Tinbergen 1954; Theil 1961), we have considered the exogenous variables as policy variables and asked the following question: Given an isolated autonomous increase in an exogenous variable by 1%, what will be the simultaneous percentage change in the endogenous variables? (See Table 12.) Assume that population (N) increases by 1 per cent by immigration, for example. Then we may expect the following reaction of the endogenous variables: the price level (P) will increase by about ⅕ per cent; nominal income (Y) will increase by more than ½ per cent; real national income (X) will increase by about ⅓ percent; employment (D) will increase by about ½ per cent; and nominal consumption (C) will increase about 9/10 per cent. Now consider an increase of nominal (money) wages (W) by 1 per cent. Such an increase may be the result of deliberate wage policy. We may expect that the price level will increase by about ¾ per cent and nominal income by about

TABLE 12

PERCENTAGE CHANGE IN ENDOGENOUS VARIABLES
WITH AN ISOLATED AUTONOMOUS INCREASE IN THE EXOGENOUS VARIABLES

ENDOGENOUS VARIABLE	EXOGENOUS VARIABLE						
	N	W	G	I	L	E	M
P	0.21	0.76	0.12	0.11	0.01	0.04	—0.03
Y	0.56	0.35	0.32	0.30	0.02	0.10	—0.08
X	0.35	—0.41	0.20	0.19	0.01	0.06	—0.05
D	0.56	—0.65	0.31	0.30	0.02	0.10	—0.08
C	0.87	0.55	0.22	0.21	0.01	0.07	—0.06

⅓ per cent; but real national income will decrease by about 4/10 per cent and employment by almost ⅔ per cent and nominal consumption will increase by about ½ per cent. What are the effects of an increase in public consumption (G) by 1 per cent? The price level will increase by more than 1/10 per cent, nominal national income by about ⅓ per cent, real national income by ⅕ per cent, employment by about 3/10 per cent, and nominal consumption by about ⅕ per cent. The consequences of an increase of nominal investment (I) by 1 per cent effected, for example, by tax policy are as follows: The price level will increase by about 1/10 per cent, nominal national income by 3/10 per cent, real national income by about ⅕ per cent, employment by 3/10 per cent, and nominal consumption by about ⅕ per cent. The effects of changes in stocks (L), imports (M), and exports (E) are very small. This shows that these variables are not very suitable for use in influencing the endogenous variables by public policy.

For the estimation of our model, data from the period 1948–60 have been used. The model is very simple, and we cannot expect great accuracy in prediction. Nevertheless, I have ventured to use the elasticities in the above table to predict the changes in the United States economy for 1963–64. Table 13 gives the actual and computed changes. Whereas there is, of course, no great accuracy in the prediction, the sign of the change and the order of magnitude has been correctly pre-

TABLE 13

UNITED STATES ECONIMIC CHANGE, 1963/64—PREDICTED AND ACTUAL
(Per Cent)

ENDOGENOUS VARIABLE	ACTUAL	PREDICTED
Price level	1.1	4.5
Nominal income.	5.9	3.1
Real income.	4.8	1.3
Employment	4.4	2.1
Nominal consumption	5.6	5.4

dicted. This shows that even such a small and simple model is perhaps not completely useless. We have presented this model only as an example. Much larger models are necessary to achieve predictions which are potentially useful in applications to economic policy.

One of the most elaborate models is the Klein-Goldberger (1955) dynamic model for the United States, 1928–52. It contains 20 endogenous variables, 20 equations, and 15 predetermined variables. Christ (1956) has applied the model for forecasts to 1953 and 1954. Apart from forecasts of investment and the price level, the forecasts of such important economic variables as national income, consumption, and employment are successful in the sense that the error of forecast is about 1 per cent, and the errors for forecasts of investment and prices are 10 and 5 per cent.

IV. Welfare Economics and Economic Policy

The Value Problem

In contrast to natural science, especially physics, economics is much more closely related to problems of applications, and its history is possibly more akin to the history of medicine. In any case it is perhaps only during the present century that "pure" or positive economics has been studied for its own sake. This is not to say, of course, that analytical propositions have not been developed by economists primarily interested in practical problems, as Schumpeter (1954) has so brilliantly shown. The orientation towards policy, especially, explains the type of economic problems which were treated by economists at any given time. But the fact that many (perhaps all) great economists were interested in problems of policy, passionately desired the adoption of certain policy measures, and perhaps even created ideologies does not mean that they did not try to apply scientific methods objectively. If we say that economics (pure or positive) should be *value free*, we mean that the economist should try to investigate objectively and in an unprejudiced way the economic phenomena. These by necessity, however, include certain valuations — for example, given preferences of the consumers. But as indicated earlier, problems of choice may also be investigated objectively by methods of mathematical economics and econometrics.

Many writers (M. Weber 1922, Weber and Topitsch 1952) have emphasized that economics should be value free. The distinction between positive and policy oriented economies is discussed by Hutchinson (1964). He especially stresses the shortcomings of modern welfare economics and also the fact that the consequences of economic policy measures must be considered in the total social framework and not as isolated economic events. Such an admonition is much more needed today than at the time of J. S. Mill when economics was less specialized and less divorced from other social sciences. The fundamental neutrality of scientific economics has been emphasized by Cairnes (1875, p. 20): "In the first place, then, you will remark that, as thus conceived, Political Economy stands apart from all particular systems of social or industrial existence. It has nothing to do with laissez faire any more than with communism." We may well agree with the view expressed by Albert (1964, p. 396):

1. In a certain sense *no science* can be value free: All sciences have a value foundation; they are influenced by valuations. 2. In a certain sense, *social sciences* cannot be value-free; they must analyze valuations in the realm of objects. 3. In a certain sense, *any science* can be value-free: no science is in need of value judgments within the context of its propositions. There is no value freedom in the absolute sense. But the methodological principle of value freedom can be maintained almost in the sense of Max Weber.

It seems obvious that we should distinguish between positive economics and economic policy which has to be based upon normative ideas. It is equally apparent that this distinction has rarely been made in the past and is indeed difficult to maintain.

Problems of Ethics

The problems of economic policy, like all political problems, involve economics in questions of ethics and social philosophy. This preoccupation can be traced back to Plato and Aristotle. It is particularly obvious in the writings of the English classical economists who were under the potent influence of utilitarian philosophy. This influence has persisted to this day. The efforts of Pareto and his modern followers and of the writers in decision theory to emancipate economics from utilitarian ethics form an important part of the background of much of the modern literature in this field. Unfortunately, logical positivists have, with a few exceptions, up to now somewhat neglected the study of ethics and politics. It seems clear, however, that methods of logical analysis are potentially important for the study of ethics (Menger 1934*b*; von Wright 1951 and 1963; Kraft 1951; Becker 1952). It is obvious that these contributions might be useful in the study of welfare economics and economic policy.

The application of *modal logic* to problems of ethics makes a study of the consistency of ethical systems possible. We present the following examples from Wright (1951, pp. 39 ff.): If doing what we ought to do commits us to do something else, then this new act is also something we ought to do. Doing the permitted can never commit us to do the forbidden. If doing something commits us to do the forbidden, we are forbidden to do the first thing. An act, which commits us to a choice between forbidden alternatives is forbidden. It is logically impossible to be obliged to choose between forbidden alternatives. Our commitments are not affected by our other obligations. If failure to commit an act commits us to perform it, then this act is obligatory. Churchman (1961) argues from a thoroughly pragmatic point of view. Basing himself upon many of the recent advances in operations research he tries to construct a science of ethics.

For the study of economic policy we might proceed in the manner of Weldon (1953). He analyses the vocabulary of politics essentially from a positivist point of view (see also von Wright 1963). Real essences, absolute standards, and the geometrical method should be recognized as illusions. Classical political theory (this includes utilitarianism and Marxism) are based upon certain metaphysical suppositions and hence are largely quite meaningless. Freedom, for instance, should be recognized as involving two concepts: free from and free to — for example, the industrial worker in a Western community at the present time, as compared to the time of Marx, is less free from interference from trade unions and government agencies, but he is more free to acquire a high living standard. It is quite senseless and not at all helpful to talk about political "foundations." This holds for democratic foundations (laissez faire liberalism), Hegelian foundations (conservativism), Marxist foundations (socialism and communism), and philosopher kings (dictatorship). The elimination of metaphysical ideas in this field, as in many other fields, would clarify the discussion of important issues. This point of view is similar to Popper's proposition regarding piecemeal engineering (Popper 1950, pp. 154 ff.).

Weldon, as well as Topitsch (1961, pp. 271 ff.), emphasizes that this critical point of view applied to traditional politics does not necessarily lead to skepticism. Extreme subjectivism and relativism in political and ethical matters is not implied. These important problems and their solution are more than mere matters of taste, but the search for absolute standards of conduct in politics cannot be justified. There are no objective standards in politics comparable to standards in physics. Judgments about ethics and politics are typically more subject to error than propositions in the natural sciences, but they are not meaningless. Appraisal statements are simply not very accurate. We may conclude that for this reason policies should always be experimental, and the danger of developing vested interest in given policies should be minimized.

Political institutions cannot always, or even usually, be completely appraised in the language of means and ends, and the same holds in aesthetics. Appraisals are empirical judgments made by individuals. There remains a *personal* component in the appraisal of political and social institutions. I would be tempted to agree with Weldon (p. 176) that we should judge such institutions according to the following criteria: Does the political system under consideration censor the reading of those who are subject to it and impose restrictions on teaching? Does it maintain that any political or other principles are immutable and therefore beyond criticism? Does it impose restrictions on the intercourse of its members with those who live under different systems? Do the rulers of the associations which have these institutions find most of their supporters among the illiterates, the uneducated, and the superstitious?

There is, of course, the danger that with the adoption of a thoroughly empirical point of view the social sciences may degenerate into conformist endeavors (Topitsch 1961; Mills 1959; Hoffmann 1961). The academic situation in the United States at the present time, where large corporations and government departments provide much employment to social scientists and also where a great deal of research in the social sciences is being supported by the government, points in this direction. Piecemeal engineering and piecemeal social technology as proposed by Popper (1950, pp. 154 ff.) may (against the wish of its originator) degenerate into a defense of the status quo. Intellectuals may become (conscious or unconscious) social managers of the existing system and their endeavors may not be much more than its ideological defense.

One may also emphasize, however, that the pressing problems of our times, the prevention of war and the economic development of the underdeveloped countries (Boulding 1964), are such that it is very doubtful if the application of piecemeal engineering would always be very helpful. For instance, the economic development of India necessitates perhaps an almost complete revolution of existing values and institutions. The transition of the retarded Indian peasant society to modern capitalism would be just as revolutionary as the transition to a Marxist dictatorship or to a mixed system, as is being attempted today. It is not easy to see how methods of slow reform can be very helpful in this connection. After all, the transition from feudalism to the modern society, which made the rise of modern science possible, was also revolutionary and painful, as Popper has repeatedly emphasized.

Welfare Economics

A tradition of doctrines of welfare economics, which is based upon the philosophy of the utilitarians (e.g., Bentham, J. S. Mill), many of whom made important contributions to positive economics, has grown up and persisted in the writings of many economists. The somewhat naive ideas of Bentham about "the greatest happiness of the greatest number" were refined and presented in very plausible form by Marshall (1948) and Pigou (1920). For an application of these ideas to Indian problems see Tintner and Patel (1966). Pareto (1927), for philosophical and political reasons, was opposed to the utilitarian point of view and proposed another method which is still in the center of discussion. The Pareto optimum is defined as the state in which no individual can be made better off without making some individual worse off. Looked at as a prescription of economic policy this amounts, of course, to a defense of the status quo.

Bergson (1948, 1954, 1966) makes a most important contribution to welfare economics. He introduces a *welfare function* which depends upon the utilities or satisfactions of *all* individuals in a given economy, but the welfare function which he proposes has been criticized by Arrow (1963; see also Rothenberg 1961 and Scitovsky 1964.)

By starting from purely individualistic and atomistic assumptions, Arrow showed that if there are at least three alternatives which the members of a society are free to order in any arbitrary way, then a social ordering must be either imposed or dictatorial. The assumption here is that choices are comparable and transitive. The welfare function is conceived in such a fashion that individual preferences are taken into account and irrelevent alternatives play no part. Dictatorship means that the choices of a single individual are decisive. Imposition means that social welfare is independent of individual choices. For a criticism of welfare economics from the extreme laissez-faire point of view see Rothbard (1956). As has been pointed out (Albert 1964), welfare economics has never really been a firm basis of economic policy (see also Robbins 1961, 1963).

The modern welfare economics considers economic phenomena in isolation. In this form modern welfare economics is decidedly inferior to the theories of the utilitarian philosophers and economists (Bentham and J. S. Mill), who considered economics as only one of the aspects of the desirable social order. Much of welfare economics was conceived as a defense of unrestricted laissez-faire. This involves, among other assumptions, the idea of consumers sovereignty — that is, each consumer is assumed to act in isolation, independently of all other consumers, to maximize his satisfaction. Whereas there is not much objection to this idea as a first approximation in the explanation of choice under static conditions, it becomes most questionable if it is made the basis of policy considerations in welfare economics. Is it really possible to consider the consumer as an independent, atomistic, and sovereign being, who ultimately determines by his choice the totality of economic phenomena? This contradicts an old idea, expressed by Aristotle, that man is "a political animal." A society of isolated atomistic individuals, as conceptualized in much of modern welfare economics, is hardly imaginable (Tintner 1946, 1960*b*).

The questionable nature of the assumption of consumer's sovereignty which is still often maintained as a foundation of welfare economics, can be indicated by an example. In an unpublished dissertation R. L. Basmann has investigated the demand for tobacco and tobacco products in the United States, 1926–45 (Tintner 1962, p. 216). He finds that the elasticity of demand for tobacco per head of population with respect to the real cost of advertising for tobacco is 0.085. If the cost of advertising for tobacco and tobacco products increases by 1 per cent, the demand for these products will increase by a little less than 1/10 per cent. This example shows how tastes and preferences of consumers are actually influenced by advertising (Chamberlin 1948). Hence it seems impossible to consider the consumer as completely sovereign and independent.

The following statement is pertinent:

A combination of the critical examination of social life and its institutions with the aid of theoretical thinking and of practical attempts to reform them by application of theoretically founded technological systems — in short, a combination of social criticism and social technology as the basis of politics — this would be the realization of the idea of approximation in social life, of approximation to a state for which there is just as little a criterion as for truth in the realm of knowledge (Albert 1964, p. 408–9).

The criticism of welfare economics by Albert (1964) is certainly not to be neglected. Perhaps we may, however, tentatively retain this idea and reform it in the direction indicated in an earlier article (Tintner 1946): take collective wants into account (Galbraith 1958, 1967), make the theory dynamic by not neglecting historical factors, perhaps introduce stochastic (i.e., probability) considerations to deal with irrational elements, and pay serious attention to external economies and diseconomies in consumption (Baumol 1965). The last point involves the fact that the individuals in the society do not really live as isolated atoms but interact, and that their preferences and tastes may be at least in part determined by this interaction.

We want to illustrate the contribution of modern mathematical economics to welfare problems by an example. The method of linear programming can be applied to short term production in general. It can make a contribution to the interesting problem of whether rational calculation and decentralized decision is possible in a static collectivist or planned economy (L. von Mises 1951). By generalizing older contributions by Pareto (1927), Barone (1935), Lange (1948), and Lerner (1944), Koopmans has shown the following: If an economic system which is essentially a generalization of the linear programming model presented above is assumed, he again proves the proposition that under free competition no firm makes any profit. But what about a collectivistic economy? Would all decisions have to be made by the central planning board? Koopmans (1951, pp. 33 ff.) proves that even under collectivism decentralized decisions are possible. Accounting or shadow prices are used in the same fashion as illustrated above. Assume also that there is a helmsman (central planning board), a custodian for each commodity, and a manager for each activity. A social optimum which corresponds exactly to the competitive optimum will be reached if in a collectivist economy the following rules are imposed: For the helmsman: choose a set of positive prices for all final commodities and inform the custodian of each commodity of this price. For the custodians: buy and sell your commodity from and to managers at a single price announced to all managers; buy all that is offered at this price; sell all that is demanded at the given price to the limit of the availability of your commodity. For all custodians of final commodities: announce the prices set on your commodity by the helmsman to managers. For all custodians of intermediary commodities: announce a tentative price on your commodity; if the demand by the managers falls short of the supply by managers, lower the prices; if demand exceeds supply, raise the price. For all custodians of primary commodities: regard the available inflow from nature as part of the supply of the commodity and then follow the rules for custodians of intermediary commodities; do not announce a price lower than zero but accept a demand below supply at zero price, if necessary. For all managers: do not engage in activities with negative (shadow) profits but maintain activities of zero profitability at a constant level and expand activities with positive profits by increasing orders for the necessary inputs with the custodians of the pertinent commodities and by offers of the outputs in question to the custodians of the commodities concerned.

This is certainly an interesting contribution of mathematical economics to one of the most important problems of our times: The theoretical possibility of collectivist economic planning. It is, however, important to realize that the result is subject to severe limitations. The theory is completely static and tells us nothing about the more important economic problems which involve time. These are, for example, economic fluctuations or economic growth and are hardly negligible in practice. Even within the subject of static economics it should be realized that the result applies to a severely idealized model of a competitive or collectivist economy. No indivisibilies are allowed. All coefficients of production are constant. There are no increasing or decreasing returns to scale. Thus if all inputs are increased in a fixed proportion, the output will also increase in the same proportion. The solution is optimal in the Pareto sense (production under unrestricted ideal free competition): no more of any final commodity can be produced, under the given assumptions, without diminishing the production of some other final commodity.

Even within the compass of the model the question of incentives is not treated. Evidently, the incentive of a capitalist entrepreneur to maximize money profits in a competitive market economy and the incentive of a manager in a collectivist economy to maximize bookkeeping profits are psychologically different. Problems of this nature are probably more adequately treated by methods of social psychology or sociology than by economics. It should be realized, however, that, perhaps in practice, there is not much difference between the manager of a large capitalist corporation and the manager of a state trust or a nationalized enterprise. It is likely that the problems faced by these managers are very similar (Schumpeter 1950), but these problems are quite different from the case analyzed by Koopmans.

It is deplorable that mathematical economists and econometricians have not occupied themselves more with one of the most important problems of our time — the question of the best economic regime, capitalism or socialism. Tinbergen's (1959, pp. 264 ff.) interesting article is one exception, which presents a promising beginning but does not come to very impressive conclusions (see also Marschak 1954).

Against this pessimistic view of welfare economics, one may maintain that the fundamental idea underlying it is a sound one, but like so many other ideas in economics it is difficult to formulate precisely and without ambiguity.

Theil's (1964) application, based upon Tinbergen's ideas (1954), of econometric methods to policy questions is without a doubt a most important contribution. These ideas are the more remarkable because the author was closely connected with government planning in the Netherlands. First, a quadratic welfare function is constructed as a rough approximation. This is based upon considerations related to the modern theory of welfare economics (Arrow 1963; Harsanyi 1955). The analogy to committee decisions is made, and a method of compromising different viewpoints is suggested. The measurable utility theory of von Neumann and Morgenstern (1944) plays a most important part. The expected value of utility is to be maximized, and certainty equivalents are introduced in order to deal with risk situations. A probability distribution is replaced by the mean value of the variable in question.

In retrospect, these ideas are applied to the economic policy of the United States 1933–6, using the Klein's model (1950). Both the static and the dynamic version of the theory are considered — that is, planning over time. There is also an application to cost minimization of a paint factory by production and employment scheduling (Holt *et al.* 1960). Finally, the theory is applied to questions of economic policy in the Netherlands 1957–9. Rothenberg (1961), who compares the essence of social decisions in a "going society" to actual choice as made in a typical family, also comes to similar conclusions. Hence, perhaps the idea of a social welfare function might be retained and even used successfully in planning for large capitalist enterprises or a whole economy.

It cannot, however, be denied that planning in Western (Theil 1961, 1964, 1966) and underdeveloped countries (Mahalanobis 1955; Schultz 1954; Tintner 1960a; Myrdal 1960) is profoundly nationalistic (Hayek 1960, p. 405). This fact in itself creates great difficulties (Robinson 1962). Except for the weaknesses of existing international organizations (Myrdal 1960), there is no reason why similar methods could not be used for international planning. It would be well for both the followers of laissez-faire capitalism and of Marxism to remember that the founders of these ideas were strong internationalists. This is as true of Karl Marx as it is of Adam Smith and David Ricardo (Robbins 1963, pp. 134 ff.). Extreme nationalism, whose growth was not anticipated by any of the writers named, has already in our century lead to two destructive world wars and seems likely to result in an even more destructive (and perhaps fatal) third war.

Welfare considerations can surely only give a partial answer to problems of economic policy. For one thing, as Albert (1964) emphasizes, economic welfare is only a part of general welfare and perhaps in some cases not even the most important part; consider, for example, the modernization of agriculture in India — surely one of the most important aspects of economic development in this country (Georgescu-Roegen 1960; Schultz 1964). In the Indian villages modernization may break up the traditional Indian society and have a number of disagreeable consequences, which cannot be overlooked in any general program.

Bibliography

AFRIAT, S. *The Cost of Living Index. Essays in Mathematical Economics. In Honour of O. Morgenstern*, ed. M. Shubik, pp. 335–66. Princeton: Princeton University Press, 1967.

AITCHESON, J., and BROWN, J. A. C. *The Lognormal Distribution.* Cambridge: Cambridge University Press, 1957.

ALBERT, A. *Social Science and Moral Philosophy*, ed. M. Bunge, pp. 385–409, 1964.

ALLAIS, M. Le Comportement de l'homme rationel devant le risque; critique des postulates et axiomes de l'école americaine, *Econometrica* 21 (1953), 503–46.

ALLEN, R. G. D. *Mathematical Analysis for Economists.* London: Macmillan, 1949.

——. *Mathematical Economics.* 2d ed., London: Macmillan, 1963.

ALT, F. Ueber die Messbarkeit des Nutzens, *Zeitschrift für Nationalokonomie* 7 (1939), 161.

ANDERSON, T. W., and RUBIN, H. Estimation of the parameters of a single equation in a complete system of stochastic equations, *Annals of Mathematical Statistics* 20 (1949), 46–63.

ARROW, K. J. *Social Choice and Individual Values.* 2d ed., New York: Wiley, 1963.

ARROW, J. K., and DEBREU, G. Existence of an equilibrium for a competitive economy, *Econometrica* 22 (1954), 265–90.

BARAN, P. A., and SWEEZY, P. M. *Monopoly Capital.* New York: Monthly Review Press, 1966.

BARONE, E. *The Ministry of Production in a Collectivist Economy*, ed. F. A. von Hayek, pp. 245–90.

BASMANN, R. L. A generalized classical method of linear estimation of coefficients in a structural equation, *Econometrica* 25 (1957), 77–83.

——. On finite sample distribution of generalized classical linear identifiability tests statistics, *Journal American Statistical Association* 55, (1960), 650–59.

BAUMOL, W. *Economic Dynamics.* 2d ed., New York: Macmillan, 1959.

——. *Economic Theory and Operations Analysis.* Englewood Cliffs, N.J.: Prentice Hall, 1961.

——. *Welfare Economics and the Theory of the State.* 2d ed., London: G. Bell, 1965.

BECKER, P. *Untersuchungen über den Modalkalkuel.* Meisenheim: Westkulturverlag, 1952.

BELLMANN, R. *Dynamic Programming.* Princeton: Princeton University Press, 1957.

BERGSON, A. *Socialist Economics*, ed. H. S. Ellis, pp. 412–48, 1948.

————. On the concept of social welfare, *Quarterly Journal of Economics* 58 (1954), 233–52.

————. *Essays in Normative Economics*. Cambridge, Mass.: Harvard University Press, 1966.

BERNADELLI, H. The origins of modern economic theory, *Economic Record* 37 (1961), 320–38.

BERNOUILLI, D. Exposition of a New Theory in the Measurement of Risk [1730], tr. L. Sommer, *Econometrica* 22 (1954), 23–36.

BLACKWELL, D. and GIRSHICK, M. A. *Theory of Games and Statistical Decisions*. New York: Wiley, 1954.

BLAUG, M. *Economic Theory in Retrospect*. Homewood, Ill.: Irwin, 1962.

BLUMEN, I., KOGAN, L. M., and McCARTHY, P. J. The industrial mobility of labor as a probabilistic process. *Cornell Studies in Industrial and Labor Relations* 7 (1955).

BOULDING, K. E. *A Reconstruction of Economics*. New York: Wiley, 1950.

————. *The Meaning of the 20th Century*. New York: Harper and Row, 1964.

BOWLEY, A. L. *Mathematical Groundwork of Economics*. Oxford: Clarendon, 1924.

BRAITHWAITE, R. B. *Scientific Explanation*. Cambridge: Cambridge University Press, 1953.

BRONFENBRENNER, M. Das Kapital for modern man, *Science and Society* 29 (1965), 419–38.

BUNGE, M. (ed.) *The Critical Approach to Science and Philosophy*. Glencoe, Ill.: Free Press, 1964.

CAIRNES, J. E. *Character and Logical Method of Political Economy*. London: Macmillan, 1875.

CARNAP, R. Testability and meaning, *Philosophy of Science* 3 (1936), 419–71.

————. Logical foundations of the unity of science, *International Encyclopedia of Unified Science* Vol. 1, No. 1, Chicago: University of Chicago Press, 1938.

————. Foundations of logic and mathematics, *International Encyclopedia of Unified Science* Vol. 1, No. 3, Chicago: University of Chicago Press, 1939.

————. *Logical Foundations of Probability*. Chicago: University of Chicago Press, 1950.

————. *The Continuum of Inductive Methods*. Chicago: University of Chicago Press, 1952.

————. *The Aim of Inductive Logic*, ed. A. Nagel, P. Suppes, and A. Tarski, pp. 303–18, 1962.

————. *My Basic Conceptions of Probability and Induction*, ed. P. A. Schlipp, pp. 966–72, 1963.

CARNAP, R., and STEGMUELLER, W. *Induktive Logik und Wahrscheinlichkeit*. Vienna: Springer-Verlag, 1958.

CHAMBERLIN, E. H. *The Theory of Monopolistic Competition*. 6th ed. Cambridge, Mass.: Harvard University Press, 1948.

CHAMPERNOWNE, D. G. A model of income distribution, *Economic Journal*, 63 (1953), 318.

CHARNES, A., and COOPER, W. W. Chance-constrained programming, *Management Science* 6 (1959), 134–48.

CHENERY, H., and CLARK, P. *Interindustry Economics*. New York: Wiley, 1959.

CHIPMANN, J. S. A survey of the theory of international trade, *Econometrica* 33 (1965), 477–519 and 685–760.

CHRIST, C. Aggregative economic models, *American Economic Review* 46 (1956), 385–408.

———. *Econometric Models and Methods*. New York: Wiley, 1966.

CHURCHMAN, C. W., ACKOFF, R. L., and ARNOFF, E. L. *Introduction to Operations Research*. New York: Wiley, 1957.

CHURCHMAN, C. W. *Prediction and Optimal Decision*. Englewood Cliffs, N.J.: Prentice Hall, 1961.

COOTNER, P. H. (ed.) *The Random Character of Stock Market Prices*. Cambridge, Mass.: Mass. Inst. Technol. Press, 1964.

CRAMÉR, H. *Mathematical Methods of Statistics*. Princeton: Princeton University Press, 1946.

DANTZIG, G. B. Programming of interdependent activities, *Econometrica* 17 (1949), 200–211.

———. Maximisation of a linear function of variables subject to linear inequalities. ed. T. C. Koopmann, pp. 339–47, 1951.

———. *Linear Programming and Extensions*. Princeton: Princeton University Press, 1963.

DAVIDSON, D. S., SIEGEL, S., and SUPPES, P. *Decision Making*. Stanford, Cal.: Stanford University Press, 1957.

DAVIS, H. T. *Theory of Econometrics*. Bloomington, Ind.: Principia Press, 1941.

DEBREU, J. *Theory of Value*. New York: Wiley, 1959.

DOMAR, E. *Essays in the Theory of Economic Growth*. New York: Oxford, 1957.

DUESENBERRY, J. S. *Income, Saving and the Theory of Consumer Behavior*. Cambridge, Mass.: Harvard University Press, 1949.

DUESENBERRY, J. S., FROMM, G., KLEIN, L. A., KUH, E., (eds.) *The Brookings Quarterly Economic Model for the United States*. Chicago: Rand McNally 1966.

DOMAR, E. *Essays in the Theory of Economic Growth*. New York: Oxford University Press, 1957.

DORFMAN, R., SAMUELSON, P. A., and SOLOW, R. N. *Linear Programming and Economic Analysis*. New York: McGraw-Hill, 1958.

ELLIS, H. S. (ed.) *A Survey of Contemporary Economics*. Philadelphia: Blakiston, 1948.

EVANS, G. C. *Mathematical Introduction to Economics*. New York: 1930.

FEIGL, H., and BRODBECK, M. (ed.) *Readings in the Philosophy of Science*. New York: Appleton-Century-Crafts, 1953.

FEIGL, H., and SELLARS, W. (ed.) *Readings in Philosophical Analysis.* New York: Appleton-Century-Crafts, 1949.

FELLNER, W. *Competition among the Few.* New York: Knopf, 1949.

FELS, E. M. About probability-like measures for entire theories, *Metrika* 7 (1963), 1–22.

FINETTI, B. DE. La Prévision; ses lois logiques, ses sources subjectives, *Annals Institut Henri Poincaré* 7 (1937), 1–68.

FISHER, F. M. On the analyis of history and independence of the social sciences, *Philosophy of Science* 27 (1960), 147–58.

———. On the cost of approximate specification in simultaneous equations estimation, *Econometrica* 29 (1961), 139–70.

———. *Dynamic Structure and Estimation in Economy Wide Econometric Models,* ed. J. S. Duesenberry *et al.* pp. 589–637, 1966.

FISHER, R. A. *Statistical Methods and Scientific Inference.* New York: Hafner, 1956.

FISZ, M. *Probability Theory and Mathematical Statistics.* 3d ed., New York: Wiley, 1963.

Fox, K. *Economic Analysis for Public Policy.* Ames, Iowa: Iowa State University Press, 1958.

FRASER, D. A. S. On fiducial inference, *Annals of Mathematical Statistics* 32 (1961), 661–76.

FRIEDMAN, M. *Essays in Positive Economics.* Chicago: University of Chicago Press, 1953.

———. *A Theory on the Consumption Function.* Princeton: Princeton University Press, 1957.

FRIEDMAN, M., and SAVAGE, L. J. The utility analysis of choices involving risk, *Journal of Political Economy* 56 (1948) 279–304.

FRISCH, R. *Statistical Confluence Analysis by Means of Complete Regression Systems.* OSLO: Universitetets Økonomiske Institutt, 1934.

GALBRAITH, J. K. *The Affluent Society.* Boston: Houghton Mifflin, 1958.

———. *The New Industrial State.* Boston: Houghton Mifflin, 1967.

GEORGESCU-ROEGEN, N. The theory of choice and constancy of economic laws, *Quarterly Journal of Economics* 54 (1950), 125–38.

———. Choice, expectations and measurability, *Quarterly Journal of Economics* 68 (1954), 503–34.

———. Economic theory and agrarian economics, *Oxford Economic Papers* 12 (1960), 1–40.

———. *Measure, quality, and optimal size.* ed. C. R. Rao pp. 231–56, 1965.

———. *Analytical Economics.* Cambridge, Mass.: Harvard University Press, 1966.

GOLDBERGER, A. S. *Econometric Theory.* New York: Wiley, 1964.

GOOD, I. J. *Probability and the Weighing of Evidence.* London: Griffin, 1950.

———. *The Estimation of Probabilities.* Cambridge, Mass.: Mass. Inst. Technol. Press, 1965.

GRAFF, J. DE V. *Theoretical Welfare Economics.* Cambridge: Cambridge University Press, 1957.

GRANGER, C. W. J., and HATAKANA, M. *Spectral Analysis of Economic Time Series*. Princeton: Princeton University Press, 1964.

GRANGER, G. G. *Méthodologie Économique*. Paris: Presses Universitaires de France, 1955.

———. *Pensée formelle et science de l'homme*. Paris: Aubier, 1960.

GREEN, H. A. J. *Aggregation in Economic Analysis*. Princeton: Princeton University Press, 1964.

GRUNBERG, E., and MODIGLIANI, F. The predictability of social events, *Journal of Political Economy* 62 (1954), 465–78.

HAAVELMO, T. The probability approach to econometrics, *Econometrica* 12 (1944), suppl.

———. *Studies in the Theory of Economic Evolution*. Amsterdam: North-Holland, 1954.

HALEY, B. F. (ed.) *A Survey of Contemporary Economics*. Vol. 2, Homewood, Ill.: Irwin, 1952.

HANNAN, E. J. *Time Series Analysis*. London: Methuen, 1960.

HARROD, F. R. *Towards a Dynamic Economics*. New York: Macmillan, 1952.

HARSANYI, J. C. Cardinal welfare, individualistic ethics, and interpersonal comparison of utility, *Journal of Political Economy*. 63 (1955), 309–21.

———. *Models for the Analysis of Balance of Power in Society*, ed. E. Nagel, P. Suppes, A. Tarski, pp. 442–62, 1962.

———. A general theory of rational behavior in game situations, *Econometrica* 34 (1966), 613–34.

HAYEK, F. A. (ed.) *Collectivist Economic Planning*. London: Routledge & Kegan Paul, 1935.

———. *The Counterrevolution of Science*. Glencoe, Ill.: Free Press, 1952.

———. *The Constitution of Liberty*. Chicago: University of Chicago Press, 1960.

HEADY, E. O., and CANDLER, W. *Linear Programming Methods*. Ames, Iowa: Iowa State University Press, 1958.

HICKS, J. R. *Value and Capital*. 2d ed., Oxford: Clarendon Press, 1946.

———. *Capital and Growth*. Oxford: Oxford University Press, 1965.

HIGGINS, B. *Economic Development*. New York: Norton, 1959.

HOFMANN, W. *Gesellschaftslehre als Ordnungsmacht*. Berlin: Duncker and Humbolt, 1961.

HOHENBALKEN, B. VON, and TINTNER, G. Econometric models for the OEEC member countries, the United States and Canada: Their application to economic policy, *Weltwirtschaftliches Archiv* 89 (1962), 29–86.

HOLT, C. C. MODIGLIANI, F., MUTH, J. F., and SIMON, H. A. *Planning, Production, Inventories and Work Force*. Englewood Cliffs, N.J.: Prentice Hall, 1960.

HOOD, W. C., and KOOPMANS, T. (eds.) *Studies in Econometric Method*. New York: Wiley, 1953.

HOUTHAKKER, H. S. Revealed preference and the utility function, *Economica* 17 (1950), 159–74.

HURWICZ, L. Conditions for economic efficiency of centralized and decentralized structures. ed. G. Grossman, *Value and Plan*. Berkeley: University of California Press, 1960.

HUTCHISON, T. W. *Positive Economics and Policy Objectives*. Cambridge, Mass.: Harvard University Press, 1964.

JEFFREYS, H. *Theory of Probability*. Oxford: Clarendon, 1948.

JEVONS, W. S. *The Theory of Political Economy*. London: Macmillan, 1911.

JOHNSTON, J. *Econometric Methods*. New York: McGraw-Hill, 1963.

KALECKI, M. A macrodynamic theory of business cycles, *Econometrica* 3 (1935), 327–44.

KANTOROVICH, L. V. Mathematical methods in the organization and planning of production (1939), *Management Science* 6 (1960), 366–422.

———. *Calcul économique et utilisation des ressources*. Paris: Dunod, 1963.

KATONA, G., KLEIN, L. R., LANSING, J. B., and MORGAN, J. N., *Contributions of Survey Methods to Economics*. New York: Columbia University Press, 1954.

KAUFMANN, F. *Methodology of Social Sciences*. New York: Oxford University Press, 1944.

KEMENY, J. G. *Carnap's Theory of Probability and Induction*. ed. P. A. Schilpp, pp. 711–38, 1963.

KEMENY, J. G., MORGENSTERN, O., and THOMPSON, G. L. A generalization of the von Neumann model of an expanding economy, *Econometrica* 24 (1956), 115–35.

KEMENY, J. G., and SNELL, J. L. *Finite Markov Chains*. Princeton, N.J.: Van Nostrand, 1960.

———. *Mathematical Models in the Social Sciences*. Boston: Ginn, 1962.

KEMENY, J. G., SNELL, J. L., and THOMPSON, G. L. *Introduction to Finite Mathematics*. New York: Prentice Hall, 1957.

KENDALL, M. G., and STUART, A. *The Advanced Theory of Statistics*. Vols. 1 and 2. New York: Hafner, 1958 and 1961.

KEYNES, J. M. *The General Theory of Employment, Interest and Money*. London: Macmillan, 1936.

———. *A Treatise on Probability*. London: Macmillan, 1948.

KEYNES, J. N. *Scope and Method of Political Economy*, 4th ed. New York: Keller, 1955.

KLEIN, L. R. *Economic Fluctuations in the United States, 1921–1941*. New York: Wiley, 1950.

———. *An Introduction to Econometrics*. Englewood Cliffs, N.J.: Prentice Hall, 1962.

KLEIN, L. R., and GOLDBERGER, A. S. *An Econometric Model for the United States, 1929–1952*. Amsterdam: North-Holland, 1957.

KNIGHT, F. H. *Risk, Uncertainty and Profit*. (reprint.) London: London School of Economics, 1933.

KOLMOGOROFF, A. *Grundbegriffe der Wahrscheinlichkeitsrechnug* Berlin: Springer-Verlag, 1933.

KOOPMANS, T. C. (ed.) *Activity Analysis of Production and Allocation*. New York: Wiley, 1951.

KOOPMANS, T. C. *Three Essays on the State of Economic Science.* New York. McGraw-Hill, 1957.

KOOPMANS, T. C., and BECKMANN, M. J. Assignment problems and the location of economic activities, *Econometrica* 25 (1957) 53–76.

KRAFT, V. *Grundlagen einer wissenschaftlichen Wertlehre* Vienna: Springer-Verlag, 1951.

KRYBURG, H. E., and SMOCKLER, H. E. *Studies in Subjective Probability.* New York: Wiley, 1964.

KUENNE, R. E. *Theory of General Equilibrium.* Princeton: Princeton University Press, 1963.

KUHN, H., and TUCKER, A., Nonlinear programming. In *Proceedings of the Second Berkeley Symposium on Mathematical Statistics and Probability,* ed. J. Neyman. Berkeley: University of California Press, 1951.

LANGE, O. *On the Economic Theory of Socialism,* ed. E. B. Lippincott, pp. 55–141, 1948.

——. *The Scope and Method of Economics.* ed. H. Feigl and M. Brodbeck pp. 744–56, 1953.

——. *Introduction to Econometrics.* London: Pergamon, 1959.

——. *Political Economy,* Vol. 1. New York: Macmillan, 1963.

LEHMANN, E. L. *Testing Statistical Hypotheses.* New York: Wiley, 1959.

LEONTIEF, W. W. *The Structure of the American Economy 1919–1939* New York: Oxford University Press, 1951.

LERNER, A. P. *The Economics of Control.* New York: Macmillan, 1944.

LESOURNE, J. *Technique économique et gestion industrielle.* Paris: Dunod, 1960.

LINDLEY, D. V. *Introduction to Probability and Statistics.* Vols. 1 and 2. Cambridge: Cambridge University Press, 1965.

LIPPINCOTT, E. B. (ed.) *On the Economic Theory of Socialism.* Minneapolis: University of Minnesota Press, 1948.

LIU, T. C. Underidentification, structural estimation and forecasting, *Econometrica* 28 (1960), 855–65.

LUCE, R. D., and RAIFFA, H. *Games and Decision.* New York: Wiley, 1957.

MACHLUP, F. The problem of verification in economics, *Southern Economic Journal* 22 (1955), 1–21.

——. *Essays on Economic Semantics.* Englewood Cliffs, N.J.: Prentice Hall, 1963.

MAHALANOBIS, P. C. The approach of operational research to planning, *Sankhya* 16 (1955), 3–130.

Malinvaud, E. Capital accumulation and efficient allocation of resources, *Econometrica* 21 (1953), 233–68.

——. *Méthodes statistiques de l'économetrie.* Paris: Dunod, 1964.

MANDELBROT, B. The Pareto-Levy Law and the distribution of income, *International Economic Review* 1 (1960), 79–106.

MARSCHAK, J. Rational behavior, uncertain prospect, and measurable utility, *Econometrica* 18 (1950), 111–41.

——. Economic measurement for policy and prediction. In *Studies in*

Econometric Method, ed. W. C. Hood, and T. C. Koopmans, pp. 1–26. New York: Wiley, 1953.

————. Towards an economic theory of organization and information. ed. Thrall, Davis, and Coombs, In *Decision Processes*, pp. 187–220. New York: Wiley, 1954.

————. *Scaling of Utility and Probability*, ed. M. Shubik, pp. 95–109, 1964.

MARSHALL, A. *Principles of Economics*. 8th ed. New York: Macmillan, 1948.

MASSÉ, P. *Le Choix des investissements*. Paris: Dunod, 1959.

MENGER, K. Das Unsicherheitsmoment in der Wertlehre. *Zeitschrift für Nationaloekonomie*. 5 (1934), 459–85.

————. *Moral, Wille und Weltgstaltung*. Vienna: Springer-Verlag, 1934*b*.

MILLS, C. W. *The Sociological Imagination*. New York: Oxford University Press, 1949.

MILNOR, J. *Games against Nature*, ed. M. Shubik, pp. 120–34, 1964.

MISES, L. VON. *Human Action*. New Haven: Yale University Press, 1949.

————. *Socialism*. New Haven: Yale University Press, 1951.

MISES, R. VON. *Wahrscheinlichkeit, Statistik und Wahrheit*. 3d ed. Vienna: Springer-Verlag, 1951.

MODIGLIANI, F. Fluctuations in the savings-income rate, *Studies in Income and Wealth* 6 (1949), New York: National Bureau of Economic Research, 1949.

MOESEKE, P. VAN. Stochastic linear programming, *Yale Economics Essays* 5 (1965), 197–254.

MOORE, H. L. *Synthetic Economics*. New York: Macmillan, 1929.

MORGENSTERN, O. Demand Theory Reconsidered, *Quarterly Journal of Economics* 62 (1947), 165–201.

————. *On the Accuracy of Economic Observations*. 2d ed. Princeton: Princeton University Press, 1963.

MORISHIMA, M. *Equilibrium, Stability and Growth*. Oxford: Clarendon, 1964.

MORRIS, C. Foundations of the theory of signs, *International Encyclopedia of Unified Science*, Vol. 1, No. 2. Chicago: University of Chicago Press, 1938.

————. *Signs, Language, and Behavior*. New York: Prentice Hall, 1946.

MOSBAEK, E. Fitting a static supply and demand function for labor, *Weltwirtschaftliches Archiv* 82 (1959), 133–46.

MOSTELLER, F., and NOGEE, P. An experimental measurement of utility, *Journal of Political Economy* 59 (1951), 371–404.

MUKHERJEE, V., TINTNER, G., NARAYANAN, R. A generalized Poisson process for the explanation of economic development, *Arthaniti* 8 (1964), 156–64.

MYRDAL, G. *Beyond the Welfare State*. New Haven: Yale University Press, 1960.

NAGEL, E. Principles of the theory of probability, *International Encyclopedia of Unified Science*, Vol. 1, No. 6. Chicago: University of Chicago Press, 1939.

NAGEL, E., SUPPES, P., TARSKI, A. (eds.) *Logic, Methodology and Philosophy of Science.* Stanford: Stanford University Press, 1962.

NASH, J. F. The bargaining problem, *Econometrica* 18 (1950) 155–62.

———. Two person cooperative games, *Econometrica* 21 (1953), 128–40.

NEUMANN, J. VON. A model of general economic equilibrium, *Review of Economic Studies* 13 (1945), 1–9.

NEUMANN, J. VON, and MORGENSTERN, O. *Theory of Games and Economic Behavior.* Princeton: Princeton University Press, 1944.

NEYMAN, J. *Lectures and Conferences on Mathematical Statistics.* Washington: Graduate School Department of Agriculture, 1938.

NORTHROP, F. S. C. *The Logic of the Sciences and the Humanities.* New York: Macmillan, 1947.

ORCUTT, G. H., GREENBERGER, M., KORBEL, J., and RIVLIN, A. M. *Microanalysis of Socioeconomic Systems.* New York: Harper & Row, 1961.

PAINLEVÉ, P. The place of mathematical reasoning in economics, ed. L. Sommer. In *Essays in European Economic Thought.* pp. 120–32. Princeton: Van Nostrand, 1960.

PAPANDREOU, A. G. *Economics as a Science.* Chicago: Lippincott, 1958.

PARETO, V. *Manual d'économie politique.* Paris: M. Giard, 1927.

PFANZAGL, J. Zur Geschichte der Theorie des Lebenshaltungsindices, *Statistische Vierteljahrsschrift* 7 (1955), 1–52.

———. *Die axiomatischen Grundlagen einer allgemeinen Theorie des Messens.* Würzburg: Physica Verlag, 1959.

PIGOU, A. C. *The Economics of Welfare.* London: Macmillan, 1920.

POPPER, K. R. *The Open Society and Its Enemies.* Princeton: Princeton University Press, 1950.

———. *The Poverty of Historicism.* New York: Harper & Row, 1957.

———. *The Logic of Scientific Discovery.* New York: Science Editions, 1961.

———. *Conjectures and Refutations.* London: Routledge & Kegan Paul, 1963a.

———. What is dialectic? (In 1963a), pp. 312–35, 1963b.

———. (1963C): Prediction and Prophecy in the Social Sciences. (In 1963a), pp. 336–46, 1963c.

PRAIS, S. J., and HOUTHAKKER, H. S., *The Analysis of Family Budgets.* Cambridge: Cambridge University Press, 1955.

QUINE, W. V. *Word and Object.* New York: Wiley, 1960.

RADNER, R. Paths of economic growth that are optimal with regard only to final states: A turnpike theorem, *Review of Economic Studies* 28 (1961), 98–104.

RAO, C. R. (ed.) *Essays in Econometrics and Planning.* Oxford: Pergamon, 1965.

RAMSEY, F. P. A. Mathematical Theory of Saving, *Economic Journal* 36 (1928), 543–59.

———. *The Foundations of Mathematics.* London: Routledge & Kegan Paul, 1931.

ROBBINS, L. *An Essay on the Nature and Significance of Economic Science.* 2d ed. London: Macmillan, 1949.

———. *The Theory of Economic Policy.* London: Macmillan, 1961.

———. *Politics and Economics.* London: Macmillan, 1963.

ROBINSON, J. *Economics of Imperfect Competition.* London: Macmillan, 1938.

———. *An Essay in Marxian Economics.* London: Macmillan, 1949.

———. *Economic Philosophy.* London: Penguin, 1962.

ROOS, C. F. *Dynamic Economics.* Bloomington, Ind.: Principia, 1934.

ROTHBARD, M. N. *Towards a Reconstruction of Utility and Welfare Economics,* ed. M. Sennholz, pp. 224–62, 1956.

ROTHENBERG, J. *The Measurement of Social Value.* Englewood Cliffs, N.J.: Prentice Hall, 1961.

SAMUELSON, P. A. A note on the pure theory of consumers behavior, *Economica* 5 (1938), 61–71 and 353–54.

———. *Foundations of Economic Analysis.* Cambridge, Mass.: Harvard University Press, 1947.

———. Consumption theory in terms of revealed preference, *Economica* 15 (1948), 243–53.

———. *The Collected Scientific Papers of Paul A. Samuelson,* Vols. 1 and 2. Cambridge, Mass.: Mass. Inst. Technol. Press, 1966.

SAVAGE, L. J. *Foundations of Statistics.* New York: Wiley, 1954.

SAVAGE, L. J. *The Foundations of Statistical Inference.* London: Methuen, 1962.

SCHLAIFFER, R. *Probability and Statistics for Business Decisions.* New York: McGraw-Hill, 1959.

SCHILPP, P. A. (ed.) *The Philosophy of Rudolf Carnap.* La Salle, Ill.: Open Court, 1963.

SCHOEFFLER, S. *The Failures of Economics.* Cambridge, Mass.: Harvard University Press, 1955.

SCHULTZ, T. W. *Transforming Traditional Agriculture.* New Haven: Yale University Press, 1964.

SCHUMPETER, J. A. *Ten Great Economists.* New York: Oxford, 1951*a.*

———. *Essays.* Cambridge, Mass.: Addison-Wesley, 1951*b.*

———. *History of Economic Analysis.* New York: Oxford, 1954.

———. *Capitalism, Socialism and Democracy,* 3d ed. New York: Harper, 1950.

SCITOVSKI, T. *Welfare and Growth.* Stanford: Stanford University Press, 1964.

SENGUPTA, J. K., and TINTNER, G. An approach to a stochastic theory of economic development with applications, *Problems of Economic Dynamics and Planning: Essays in honour of M. Kalecki,* pp. 373–93. Warsaw: Polish Scientific Publishers, 1964.

———. Some aspects of trend in the aggregative models of economic growth, *Kyklos* 16 (1963), 47–61.

SENGUPTA, J. K., TINTNER, G., and MORRISON, B., Stochastic linear programming with applications to economic models, *Economica* 30 (1963), 262–76.

SENNHOLZ, M. (ed.) *Freedom and Free Enterprise.* Princeton: Von Nostrand, 1956.

SHONFIELD, A. *Modern Capitalism.* New York: Oxford University Press, 1965.

SHUBIK, M. *Strategy and Market Structure.* New York: Wiley, 1959.

SHUBIK, M. (ed.). *Game Theory and Related Approaches to Social Behavior.* New York: Wiley, 1964.

SIEVERS, A. M. *Revolution, Evolution and the Economic Order.* Englewood Cliffs, N.J.: Prentice Hall, 1962.

SIMON, H. A. *Models of Man.* New York: Wiley, 1957.

SOLOMON, H. (ed.) *Mathematical Thinking in the Measurement of Behavior.* Glencoe, Ill. Free Press, 1960.

STEINDL, J. *Random Processes and the Growth of Firms.* New York: Hafner, 1965.

STIGLER, G. J. *Five Lectures on Economic Problems.* London: Longmans Green, 1949.

————. The development of utility theory, *Journal of Political Economy* 58 (1950), 307–27, 373–96.

STONE, R. On the interdependence of blocks of transactions, *Journal Royal Statistical Society* Suppl. 8 (1947), 1.

————. *The Role of Measurement in Economics.* Cambridge: Cambridge University Press, 1951.

————. Three models of economic growth. ed. E. Nagel, P. Suppes, and A. Tarski, pp. 494–506, 1962.

STROTZ, R. H., and WOLD, H. Recursive *vs.* nonrecursive systems: An attempt of a synthesis, *Econometrica* 28 (1960), 417–27.

THEIL, H. *Linear Aggregation of Economic Relations.* Amsterdam: North-Holland, 1954.

————. *Economic Forecasts and Policy,* 2d ed., Amsterdam: North-Holland, 1961.

————. *Alternative Approaches to the Aggregation Problem,* ed. E. Nagel, P. Suppes, and A. Tarski, pp. 507–27, 1962.

————. *Studies in Mathematical and Managerial Economics.* Amsterdam: North-Holland, 1964.

————. *Applied Economic Forecasting.* Amsterdam: North-Holland, 1966.

————. *Economics and Information Theory.* Amsterdam: North-Holland, 1967.

THRALL, R. M., COOMBS, C. H., and DAVIS, R. L. (eds.) *Decision Processes.* New York: Wiley, 1954.

TINBERGEN, J. *On the Theory of Economic Policy.* Amsterdam: North-Holland, 1954.

————. *Selected Papers.* Amsterdam: North-Holland, 1959.

TINTNER, G. The theory of choice under subjective risk and uncertainty, *Econometrica* 9 (1941), 298–304.

————. The theory of production under nonstatic conditions, *Journal of Political Economy* 50 (1942*a*), 645–67.

————. A contribution to the non-static theory of choice, *Quarterly Journal of Economics* 56 (1942*b*), 274–306.

————. A contribution to the nonstatic theory of production, ed. Lange,

O., McIntyre, F., and Yntema, Th., *Studies in Mathematical Economics and Econometrics.* Chicago: University of Chicago Press, 1942c.

————. A note on welfare economics, *Econometrica* 14 (1946), 69–78.

————. Foundations of probability and statistical inference, *Journal of the Royal Statistical Society* Ser. A, 112 (1949), 251–79.

————. *Econometrics* New York: Wiley, 1952.

————. The definition of econometrics, *Econometrica* 21 (1953a), 31–40.

————. *Mathematics and Statistics for Economists.* New York: Rinehart, 1953b.

————. Einige Grundprobleme der Oekonometrie, *Zeitschrift für die gesamte Staatswissenschaft* 111 (1955), 601–10.

————. Game theory, linear programming and input-output analysis, *Zeitschrift für Nationaloekonomie* 17 (1957), 1–38.

————. The application of decision theory to a simple inventory problem, *Trabajos de Estadistica* 10 (1959), 239–47.

————. A note on stochastic linear programming, *Econometrica* 28 (1960a), 490–95.

————. External economies in consumption. *Essays in Economics and Econometrics*, pp. 107–112. Chapel Hill: University of North Carolina Press, 1960b.

————. *Handbuch der Oekonometrie.* Berlin: Springer-Verlag, 1960c.

————. Eine Anwendung der Wahrscheinlichkeitstheorie von Carnap auf ein Problem der Unternehmungsforschung, *Unternehmungsforschung* 4 (1960d), 164–70.

————. The use of stochastic linear programming in planning, *Indian Economic Review* 5 (1960e), 159–67.

————. *Mathématiques et statistiques pour les économistes.* Paris: Dunod, 1962.

————. Lineare Programme und Input-Output Analyse, *Statistische Hefte* 5 (1965), 50–55.

————. Modern decision theory. *Journal of the Indian Society of Agricultural Research Statistics* 18 (1966), 82–98.

TINTNER, G., and MURTEIRA, B. Un modelo input-output simplificado para a economia portuguesa. *Colectanea de Estudos*, No. 8. Lisbon: Centro de Estudos de Estadistica Economica, 1960.

TINTNER, G., and PATEL, R. C. A long-normal diffusion process applied to the economic development of India, *Indian Economic Journal* 13 (1966), 465–75.

TINTNER, G., and MURTEIRA, B. Um modelo input-output simplificado para nal of Farm Economics 48 (1966), 704–10.

TINTNER, G., and PÁTEL, R. C. A log-normal diffusion process applied to Theory of Stochastic Processes to Economic Development. The Theory and Design of Economic Development, ed. I. Adelman and E. Thorbeck, pp. 99–110. Baltimore: Johns Hopkins, 1966.

TINTNER, G., and THOMAS, E. J., Un modèle stochastique de développement économique avec application à l'industrie anglaise *Revue d'Economie Politique* 73 (1963), 278–80.

TOPITSCH, E. *Vom Ursprung und Ende der Metaphysik*, Vienna: Springer-Verlag, 1958.

————. *Sozialphilosophie zwischen Ideologie und Wissenschaft*. Neuwied: Luchterhand, 1961.

VADJA, S. *Mathematical Programming*. Reading, Mass.: Addison-Wesley, 1961.

VINER, J., ADAM SMITH and laissez-faire, *Journal of Political Economy* 35 (1927), 198–232.

WALD, A. The approximate determination of indifference systems by means of Engel curves, *Econometrica* 8 (1940), 144–75.

————. *Statistical Decision Functions*. New York: Wiley, 1950.

————. On some systems of equations of mathematical economics, *Econometrica* 19 (1951), 368–403.

WEBER, M. *Gesammelte Aufsätze zur Wissenschaftslehre*. Tübingen: Mohr, 1922.

WEBER, W., and TOPITSCH, E. Das Wertfreiheitsproblem seit Max Weber, *Zeitschrift für Nationaloekonomie* 13 (1952), 199.

WELDON, T. D. *The Vocabulary of Politics*. London: Penguin, 1953.

WICKSELL, K. *Lectures on Political Economy*, Vol. 1. London: Routledge & Kegan Paul, 1934.

WIENER, N. *God and Golem*. Cambridge, Mass.: Mass. Inst. Technol. Press, 1964.

WHITTLE, P. *Prediction and Regulation*. London: English Universities Press, 1963.

WILKS, S. S. *Mathematical Statistics*. New York: Wiley, 1962.

WOLD, H. *A Letter report to Professor P. C. Mahalanobis*, Rao, R. C., ed., pp. 309–328, 1965.

WOLD, H., and JUREÉN, L. *Demand Analysis*. New York: Wiley, 1953.

WRIGHT, G. H. VON *An Essay in Modal Logic*. Amsterdam: North-Holland, 1951.

————. *The Logic of Preference*. Edinburgh: Edinburgh University Press, 1963*a*.

————. *The Varieties of Goodness*. London: Routledge & Kegan Paul, 1963*b*.

ZEUTHEN, F. *Problems of Monopoly and Economic Welfare*. London: Routledge & Kegan Paul, 1933.

ZWEIG, F. *Economic Ideas*. Englewood Cliffs, N.J.: Prentice Hall, 1950.